Wholistic Psychology

Wholistic Psychology

To Revolutionize the Mindset Supporting the
Trumpism of Materialistic Society

FRANCES GRACE ROGERS

ISBN: 1978242204
ISBN 13: 9781978242203

I see a fulfillment of the great law of all worlds, that
while the wisdom of man thinks it is working one
thing, the wisdom of nature constrains it to work another and quite a different and far better thing.

Edwin A. Abbott

What has been spoiled through [human] fault can
be made good again through [human] work. It is not
immutable fate . . . that has caused the state of cor-
ruption, but rather the abuse of human freedom.

Richard Wilhelm, *I Ching*

Science is not only compatible with spirituality; it is a profound source of spirituality.

Carl Sagan

Table of Contents

Music composed and performed by the author is available to the public at soundcloud.com/the-emergent-mind

Introduction

FOR YEARS, MANY liberal people have known the need to reform the political and religious affairs that have produced our predominantly shallow, spiritless, and violent human world.

The election of Donald Trump as president of the so-called land of the free has brought that need to the surface even more so than George W. Bush's administration that advanced the deterioration toward fascism.[1]

While some describe Trump as a narcissist and sociopath, his extremity, evidenced in lack of empathy or remorse, moves his functioning to that of a psychopath, which is having murderous results: supporting the underlying right-wing denial of the human right for health care; refusal to work to save our life sustaining planet; advocating hate crimes and the oppression of women. He was voted into office by conservatives holding traditional attitudes in politics and religion. It is probable that many of those conservatives are also complacent people—"self-satisfaction especially when accompanied by unawareness of actual dangers or deficiencies."[2]

That lack of awareness is actually lack of consciousness. Nobel laureate, neuropsychologist, neurobiologist Roger Wolcott Sperry addresses the refusal to consider that lack of consciousness of spatial right brain mental forces in the field of psychology:

"This is the general stance of modern behavioral science out of which comes today's prevailing objective, mechanistic, materialistic, behavioristic, fatalistic, reductionist view of the nature of mind and psyche. This kind of thinking is not confined to our laboratories and the classrooms, of course. It leaks and spreads, and though never officially imposed on the societies of the Western world, we nevertheless see the pervasive influence of creeping materialism everywhere we turn."[3]

The field of psychology definitely has an underlying presence in all of society, including our educational systems, also infiltrated by complacency.

Regarding the reductionist view, a turnaround from the reductionist direction that most sciences have taken is described in James Gleick's *Chaos; Making a New Science.*[4] That science is revolutionary, essentially unifying many sciences. Those top-down scientists evidenced the spatial brain attribute of seeing the big picture—holistic view. They were also intuitive, for they had an eye for pattern, especially patterns that appeared on different scales at the same time. Scaling systems is a concept that also applies to society. Those Chaos scientists' work was derided by many in the scientific community. Glieck's assessment is one that is agreeable to explain that derision: "Shallow ideas can be assimilated; ideas that require people to reorganize their picture of the world provoke hostility."

Psychology is generally accepted as the science that studies the human mind and behavior. It is truly a sick field when the functions of the amazing human brain have been ignored, especially the findings of Roger Wolcott Sperry regarding the functioning of the right and left hemispheres. He has encountered the same problem those

Chaos scientists did. Sperry's accomplishments do, indeed, require many people, especially in the field of psychology, to reorganize their picture of the human world and the functions of the human mind, including their own.

It has also been known for many years that the system of psychology/psychiatry needs to be revolutionized. Psychiatrist Thomas S. Szasz addresses that need in his book, *The Myth of Mental Illness.*[5]

It became evident to me in graduate school that the field of psychology is not scientific but comparable to religion with its numerous denominations based on the beliefs of the theorists. The psychological bible, *Diagnostic Statistical Manual: Mental Disorders,* as well, has nothing to do with science, for its concepts essentially consider symptoms as the disease.

There are, however, some scientists, like neuroendocrinology's Robert Sapolsky, bordering on the field of psychology, who can contribute to that revolution. It is evident in Sapolski's writings as well as his 2008 documentary, *Stress, Portrait of a Killer.* He is also a major spokesman in the 2011 documentary, *Zeitgeist, Moving Forward,* which includes a protest against the biological deterministic belief that behavior is genetic—the fatalism to which Sperry was referring.

Sperry's scientific findings regarding dual brain functioning gives credence to the functions of this author's mind after a creative illness that began in January, 1990. *Creative Illness* is a phrase coined by Psychiatrist Henri F. Ellenberger: "It occurs in various settings and is to be found among shamans, among the mystics of various religions, in certain philosophers and creative writers."[6] Mine, however, evoked an awakening of my higher spatial right brain capabilities on August 6, 1991, the 48th anniversary of my birth, a date that had symbolic meaning for me—Life is a Gift. The major source of that awakening was many years of experience working as a mental health counselor. Clients taught me more about human thought, emotion, and behavior than any theory addressed in my education.

After my awakening—a life-altering experience—I turned to the true sciences in an attempt to understand what was happening to my mind. There was nothing in the field of psychology to address it other than what Carl Jung termed, "the coming of the unconscious."[7] It was truly serendipitous to discover Sperry in Betty Edwards' book, *Drawing on the Right Side of the Brain*,[8] in 1995.

Many years of ongoing research, insights, and evolution of consciousness resulted in my 2016 book, *Empowered Humans: The Phenomenon of Being*, regarding the human capacity for wholeness and balance. It included knowledge, shared by example, especially the process of overcoming the man-made impediments to wholeness, as well as fulfilling my creative spatial brain talents of musical compositions and art. Essentially it was the culmination of enlightenment, including the wisdom of nature.

Human wisdom is defined as the ability to discern or judge what is true, right, or lasting; insight. It also includes common sense and good judgment as well as the sum of learning through the ages; knowledge. It can be found in the wise teachings of the ancient sages.[9]

Sage is an old term used to represent people who were practical, intuitive, and insightful, gaining wisdom through introspection and experience. True sages, as distinguished from the exploitative nature of gurus or the sorcerous traits of shamans, were Humanists who believed in humanity's potential to make positive changes as well as the wisdom of nature.

Wisdom has always been congruent with nature as well as the sciences that have advanced our knowledge of the functions of nature. Humanity is not separate from but an interconnected part of nature.

Also included in *Empowered Humans* was the discovery that knowledge regarding the functions of the dual hemispheres of the human brain, as well as the human connection with nature, has been known by insightful humans for thousands of years prior to the man-made conception of religion. That monotheist god was conceived approximately five thousand years ago to gain power and control over other people, especially women; religion and patriarchy are inextricably intertwined. The result has become oppression—unjust or cruel exercise of authority or power. Oppression, in any form, is evil.

The election of Donald Trump as president of the U.S. invoked the consideration to expand the contents of my previous book. The necessity for this writing, though, became obvious after an encounter with the psychology department at Rollins College, Winter Park, Florida, where I achieved my BS degree. I protested, in writing, the announced course at the 2017 Alumni meeting, "The Right Brain/Left Brain Myth," which served to confirm that the field of psychology continues to contribute to our unbalanced human world, as well as the numerous unbalanced people working in the field. The written response received was proof perfect that psychology contains no valid science. That letter, as well, confirmed the fact that it is complacency which maintains that lack of balance.

The source of encouragement was Betty Edwards who expressed her thoughts regarding my previous achievements, "….happy to know that a strong advocate is working hard to put things right. Many people these days are denying the work of Sperry and others, and we see all around us the triumph of the left brain. But there are others, like you and perhaps myself, who are knocking at the foundations and will eventually be heard."

Regarding the title, *wholistic* is used rather than *holistic*, for the treatise goes far beyond mind, body, and spirit, generally addressed in healing systems considered to be alternative.

The first part of Chapter 1 moves backward in time, not only to expound the history of those ancient enlightened humans, but to elaborate the source of oppression. The second part addresses the continued deterioration of human systems. Knowledge of the underlying source is necessary in order to bring reformation.

The second Chapter includes self-actualization, the highest of human callings, attained by modern sages who have advanced human knowledge of the wisdom of nature, including Sperry. His discoveries regarding the human potential to reflect that wisdom is essential to revolutionizing the mindset of psychology, as well as promoting balance and harmony of our human systems at large. Also included in Chapter 2 is this author's conception of the multidimensional reflective human, basic to Wholistic Psychology.

The third Chapter exposes the current pathology of psychology and the many issues that need to be reformed, especially that massive left brain ego—basic to Trumpism—which is evidenced throughout the field. It permeates practically all of human society on every scale, the familial, community, state, national, and even global systems.

The fourth Chapter advances knowledge of the functions of the sequential left brain and the spatial right brain, basic to an explanation of the depravity imposed by left brain conservatives. It also includes proposed changes in our educational systems that would promote consciousness of higher spatial brain capabilities, challenging the ignorance and lack of consciousness which supports that depravity.

The fifth Chapter elaborates this author's hope for positive change so needed in this world. It also includes some of my experiences as a mental health counsellor which resulted in the creative illness, subsequent awakening, and ongoing evolution of consciousness. The creative illness essentially evoked directives for self-knowledge, as well as exposing the man-made impediments to self-actualization—the bringing to actual one's whole self. It also includes some of my oppressive personal history that was resolved through introspection and self-knowledge.

Ellenberger, in addition to his creative illness term, asserts that a psychological theorist's personal history is a major contribution to theories evoked, with which I am in total agreement. Actually that is evident regarding many fields, including scientists. It is the reason the backgrounds of many of the individuals in this writing are addressed, as well as their theories.

1

Pertinent Human History
Golden Ages Impeded by Patriarchy

CARBON DATING, DISCOVERED in the late 1940s, changed archaeology and updated knowledge regarding human development. Stephen Jay Gould, paleontologist, evolutionary biologist, and historian of science, authored ten books regarding his significant findings. His book, *The Mismeasure of Man*[10] can be a major contribution to the revolution of psychology.

Throughout that book he reveals the subjectivity of the so-called scientists who were, and continue to be, the source of that mismeasurement, especially the selfish gene centered view of behavior promoted by authors Richard Dawkins and Stephen Pinker. Those two men exhibit massive egos and bring increase to no one but themselves. Both Dawkins and Pinker contribute to our spiritless world by supporting "Darwinian inequities,"[11] which results in classification of people and a materialistic and fractious society.

Gould's paleontology reveals that the human brain has not changed in over 40,000 years. In other words, after billions of years of evolution from the simplest life forms, humans reached biological maturity. Other archaeological findings support Gould's work:

musical instruments made 42,000 years ago in Germany; the *Cave of Forgotten Dreams*, in France, produced over 30,000 years ago. The phenomenal art, painted on the walls of the cave, essentially tells stories; also in that cave are sculptures honoring the female body.

Gould also knew that we are inextricably part of nature and human uniqueness resides primarily in our brains; human societies change by cultural evolution, not as a result of biological alterations. He stated that "'nothing but' an animal is as fallacious a statement as 'created in God's own image.'"

Examples of cultural evolution are evidenced in ancient Egypt and China, during periods of peace, harmony, stability, and prosperity. Ancient Egypt's newly discovered history is available in the 2009 documentary series titled *The Pyramid Code*. Pertinent is *The Empowered Human*, the 4th in that series; its focus is the proposition that the pyramids were the product of a Golden Age in Egypt. Many Egyptians fulfilled the human potential for wholeness and balance in their refined senses and higher levels of consciousness, which evoked superior abilities. The evidence of a utopian possibility is exhibited in hieroglyphs recorded during the period 10,000-3,000 BCE. Those hieroglyphic writings suggest that the pyramids are much older than previously known, and that Golden Age was governed by a balanced society with equality of the sexes and respect for all life.

Those hieroglyphic images reveal those ancient Egyptians' awareness of the spatial and sequential brain attributes and the contralateral arrangement: the left hemisphere controls the right side of the body, and the right hemisphere controls the left side of the body. Those hemispheric attributes were known to be complimentary and existing in both men and women. The mind-body connection was valued, and they were even aware of senses that go beyond sensate existence. Their creativity was evidenced, not only in those hieroglyphs but in their beautiful artifacts.

Those Ancient Egyptians also evidenced awareness of the connections between humans and the gods [creative forces] of nature, like the sun god. As we all know now, the sun is a fundamental force of life on planet earth. Yet the human spirit—that cosmic life force—was an enigma, just as it is today. Primarily, that empowering energy was associated with cosmology, which evolved to the conception of what is now known as astrology, the pseudo-science of the cosmos. Paradoxically, those astrological concepts became basic to many of the myths in religion, e.g. Virgo associated with the virgin birth.[12]

That balanced period belies any historical assumption that the pyramids were built by slaves. Instead, it is evidenced that those workers lived comfortably with human needs met.

A major shift in Egyptian culture was noted in approximately 3,000 BCE. The hieroglyphics produced then were reflective of patriarchy and a movement toward violence and oppression: wars, slavery, and the sex slaves women became in the Pharaohs' harems. Carmen Boulter, the director and the major spokesperson of the film, through her rhetoric (persuasion) and hermeneutics (interpretations), asserts that the shift to patriarchy was instigated by the spiritual leaders who used their positions to gain power.

Repeatedly Boulter refers to historical Egyptology as being "seen through the eyes of patriarchy." That view is little more misleading than seeing through the eyes of a woman who upholds shamans, the use of hallucinogenic drugs, and holds the ridiculous egotistic belief that she is a reincarnated ancient Egyptian. She did not address that belief in the film. I found it in an article regarding her personal life, for I knew, intuitively, that something was amiss. Boulter is a prime example of one whose subjectivity underlies most of her rhetoric and hermeneutics as well as sustaining human myth, e.g., the shaman based myth of chakras. Myth is in total conflict with science or wisdom attained by insight.

The use of those hallucinogenic drugs do, however, provide some explanation for the decline in consciousness; those *bad trips* into the underworld, contributing to the myths of life after death. Hallucinogens also suppress higher levels of mental functioning, damage that can be permanent. Without the cerebrum's sequential and spatial brain functioning, humans are no more conscious than animals, and, in many instances, exhibit animal behavior in sex and aggression.

Another disturbing spokesman is Graham Hancock who is obsessed with the supernatural, as though nature and its laws are not good enough for him. The supernatural is simply an attempt to explain something one does not understand.

The Egyptian spokesman in that film asserts that the concepts conceived during that balanced period remained in the subculture of Egyptian society. Moving forward in time, that assertion is an explanation for another man's conception of balance—Jesus; it is evident in the Gnostic Gospel of Thomas, particularly the specialized functions of the dual hemispheres and the contralateral arrangement.

Also, the shift to patriarchy becomes validated with Moses' writing of the Pentateuch. By the time Moses entered the picture, patriarchy was well established, and those pharaohs had set themselves up as gods. Raised in a harem as an Egyptian prince, the only father he knew was the ruling Pharaoh, some say Ramses II.

The Pentateuch, the five books of the Torah, is maintained in Islam tradition and in the Old Testament of the Christian Bible. Moses invented that monotheistic god in an image strikingly similar to his Pharaoh father, a jealous god, particularly jealous of women's capacity to give birth as well as jealous of those gods [creative forces] of nature.

As said before, Gould knew that the human forebrain, the highly evolved spatial and sequential hemispheres, is what distinguishes humans from other animals. When the higher hemispheric functioning is suppressed or lacking in development, it opens the door to instincts common to all animals, that fight-flight reaction as well as animalistic male dominance—the instinct to procreate and insure his own paternity. That animalism is evident in those Egyptian harems conceived to insure the Pharaoh's paternity. It was substantiated in the Book of Genesis with women created as the second sex to pleasure men and to procreate. Eating the fruit of the tree of knowledge of good and evil was condemned—the introduction to complacency—necessary to maintain those myths. If one does attain that knowledge, one knows that it was humans who created evil and how destructive the concept of that jealous god—invented in man's image—actually is. That concept has moved much of humanity away from reality.

That jealous god is evident in the story of Cain and Abel with the preference for animal offerings over the fruits of the land, setting brother against brother; the result was murder. That story still lives today in the not-so-civil wars in the Middle East where Abraham's lineage from his harem became divided by jealousy. Animalistic sex and aggression continues in the 21st century in Muslim countries where even females' intellect is condemned by forbidding their education.

That jealous god myth continued when, in Christian history, he morphed into the devil (satan) and the first known Jekyll and Hyde. It becomes obvious when man projected his own evil onto the fruit of women's womb—the concept of original sin. Without that concept and that devil myth, the whole of Christianity falls apart. There is no need for a savior, and man has himself to blame for the evils that do exist.

Thomas Paine, an 18th century writer, political activist, philosopher, and revolutionary had a similar response and said it more succinctly: "Whenever we read the obscene stories, the voluptuous debaucheries, the cruel and tortuous executions, the unrelenting vindictiveness with which more than half the Bible is filled, it would be more consistent that we call it the word of a demon than the word of God. It is a history of wickedness that has served to corrupt and brutalize mankind."[13]

Man is to blame for the evils that do exist in the myths they have concocted. Nobel Laureate Bertrand Russell, another philosopher who believed in freedom of thought and humanitarian ideals, maintained that religion, despite any positive effects it may have, "serves to impede knowledge, foster fear and dependency, and is responsible for much of the war, oppression, and misery of the world."[14]

In contrast to those myths are Jesus' teachings in the Gnostic Gospel of Thomas. Marvin Meyer is regarded as a foremost scholar of Gnosticism. The Gnostic texts were originally known as the Nag Hammadi Library discovered in 1945, buried in southern Egypt. Meyer's expertise is enlightening in his book, *The Gnostic Gospels of Jesus.*[15] Regarding Gnosticism in general, Meyer says: "In Gnostic texts, unlike gospels of the cross [the first four gospels in the New Testament], knowledge is more important than faith, and knowledge of oneself leads to salvation." Meyer's analysis of the Gnostic book of the Great Invisible Spirit and Secret Book of John results in his thought that the unfolding of the divine One is as much a story about psychology as it is about mythology and metaphysics: "the expressions of the divine One are mental capabilities—mind (nous), forethought (pronoia), thought (enoia), insight (epinoia), wisdom (sophia), even mindlessness (aponoia)."

Meyer reveals that *The Gospel of Thomas* is different from other Gnostic writings, for Jesus is portrayed as imparting wisdom in dialogue. In that gospel there is no mention of physical miracles, fulfilling prophecy, apocalyptic warning, nor does Jesus place himself above those around him except as an example.

The following excerpts are pertinent: "If your leaders say to you, 'Look, the kingdom is in heaven,' then the birds of heaven will precede you. If they say to you 'It is in the sea,' then the fish will precede you. Rather, the kingdom is inside you and it is outside you." (3: 1-3) "Know what is in front of your face, and what is hidden from you will be disclosed to you." (5: 1) "When you make the two into one, you will become children of humankind." (106) What *the two* refers to is answered in Jesus' response to a question posed to him regarding entering the kingdom of heaven: "When you make eyes in place of an eye, a hand in place of a hand, a foot in place of a foot, an image in place of an image, then you will enter." (22) To use both eyes and experience that contra-lateral arrangement is obvious.

Closely related and supportive of the synthesis of both spatial and sequential capabilities is another maxim by Jesus: "… I say if one is whole, one will be filled with light, but if one is divided, one will be filled with darkness." (61: 5)

Jesus acknowledges intuition as a blessing; he makes numerous references to self-examination. The more familiar prescription by Jesus about clearing up one's vision can be found in the biblical *Gospel of Matthew* as well as *The Gospel of Thomas*: "You see the speck that is in your sibling's eye, but you do not see the beam that is in your own eye. When you take the beam out of your eye, then you will see clearly to take the speck out of your sibling's eye." (26: 1)

As to the creative potential, his knowledge is reflected in his words: "Do not let your right hand know what your left hand is doing." (62: 2) He is prohibiting the egotistic tendency to filter out spatial brain capabilities which threaten one's beliefs, and/or to interpret any experience through the fog of prejudice or dogma.

Jesus, as portrayed by Thomas, was opposed to dogma that closes the door to new knowledge and gave few commandments. In addition to the one regarding creativity, he said, "Do not lie" (6: 2) and "Be on guard against the world." (21: 6) In response to the question, "When will the kingdom come?" Jesus said, "It will not come by watching for it. It will not be said 'Look, here it is,' or 'Look, there it is.' Rather, the father's kingdom is spread out upon the earth, and people do not see it." (113: 3, 4)

Enmeshed in that belief of the father god, though, bestial hostility and aggression is revealed in his statement, "Perhaps people think that I have come to impose peace upon the world. They do not know that I have come to impose conflicts on the earth: fire, sword, war." (19: 1, 2).

▲ ▲ ▲

The Golden Age in China was achieved by the Shang dynasty in the Yellow River Valley—the cradle of Chinese civilization—during the second millennium BCE. Women, during that period, enjoyed a higher and better status than in any other time of China's history. Toward the end of the Shang Dynasty, the *I Ching* was conceived by a group of sages. It is the only book of its kind, for all of the metaphors are based on nature. Like those ancient Egyptians, those sages were cognizant of the spatial and sequential hemispheres of the human brain. The spatial brain, called the Creative Yang force, associated with heaven [the cosmos], and the sequential brain, the Receptive Yin force, associated with the earth, constitute the primary forms of the six line hexagrams throughout the book. The balance between the two is a major value addressed in the hexagram *Modesty* in which there is nothing extreme. Extremity, in any form, does not further balance; it frequently brings on arrogance. The balance between the two modes of functioning is also addressed regarding the hexagram of *Peace*. It is in a commentary regarding that hexagram that the dual hemispheres are addressed, "… the movement of yang is thought of as being toward the right and that of yin toward the left."

As said in the Introduction, those sages were distinctly different from shamans in that they gained wisdom through introspection and experience. They were Humanists due to that introspection. Renowned mythologist Joseph Campbell confirms it in *The Hero's Journey* regarding people who examined their lives, "Where we thought to travel outward, we shall come to the center of our own existence. And where we thought to be alone, we shall be with all the world."[16] Those sages placed great emphasis on the values of honesty and sincerity, compassion, wisdom, justice, human dignity, and virtuous character. They focused, as well, on the spirit—the ascending force in nature and humans. Confucius' assessment of the *I Ching* was that it is a Book of Wisdom, not a divining tool to predict one's future.

That Golden Age in China ended though, for patriarchy crept in from the West. According to Pedro Ccinos Arcones, "…..it came with people speaking Indo-European languages and was reflected in the influence on the Zhou Kings that defeated the Shang Dynasty and started the oppression of women in China." [17]

Those new Zhou Kings altered the *I Ching* by imposing layers of patriarchal interpretations. The Spatial Creative Yang force was redefined as masculine and the Sequential Yin force as feminine, placing women in the submissive role beneath the powerful male. Like Egyptian Pharaohs, those patriarchal Chinese leaders made sex slaves, called concubines, an institutional part of that culture. Even in the altered *I Ching,* awareness of scaling systems is evidenced; the functions of the family reflects the beliefs of the systems at large. Women in the common household who fulfilled their submissive roles were considered ideal.

One of the most popular Western interpretations is Richard Wilhelm's *I Ching or Book of Changes.* His first 1924 publication was in German. Carl Baynes' initial English translation was published in 1950 and republished many times since then. A more recent rendition is by Taoist Master Alfred Juang, *The Complete I Ching.*[18] Both books are not only contaminated by patriarchy but by their author's subjectivity. That contamination is obvious when comparing what Juang claims to be the original poems, which he includes in his book, with his interpretations. He is fully enmeshed in the traditions of the Zhou Dynasty.

Richard Wilhelm's use of the word *god* for the spirit is also an example. That word, with all its implications, does not exist in those supposedly original poems. Wilhelm's belief in Christianity is evident when he footnotes biblical references to Jesus, distorting the original concepts to fit with his beliefs.

I discovered Wilhelm's interpretation in 1994. I found it worth the effort to see through that subjectivity, not only to discern the wisdom and humane values, but various hexagrams substantiated many of the poems evoked during my creative illness, especially one regarding the human spirit—the ascending power within.

Deterioration to the Big Divide: Flatland and Spaceland

In his Introduction to *The Mismeasurement of Man,* Gould addresses the prejudices, including religion and that male god, underlying the biological determinists' gene centered view of behavior. Those biological determinists invoked the traditional prestige of science as objective knowledge to support their prejudices, e.g., blacks are a separate race from whites, inheritance of intelligence … and the falsity of that so-called science. In his Acknowledgments Gould even addresses the sexist title of his book as a commentary on the biological determinists. "They did indeed study 'man' (that is, white European males), regarding this group as a standard and everybody else as something to be measured unfavorably against it. That they mismeasured 'man' underscores the double fallacy."

Gould also comments on Daniel J. Kelves' book, *In the Name of Eugenics,*[19] "The finest of all books on the history of eugenics." Kelves also addresses the social prejudices within that field as well as the destruction of humans in the name of eugenics, including the holocaust. In that book, JBS Haldane's 1924 opposition is evident in his complaint that genetic theory was being used in Britain "to support the political opinions of the extreme right and in America by some of the most ferocious enemies of human liberty."

The political right, which resists change, is associated with the sequential left brain, and the political left, which furthers change, is associated with the spatial right brain. The extreme right is comparable to fascism; the extreme left is comparable to anarchy. Extremism does not further balance. Politics is the result of the big divide between the sequential and spatial brains imposed by human constructionism.

Pertinent to the extreme right use of that genetic theory to maintain control over society in nineteenth century England is the creative illness and subsequent awakening of master teacher, theologian, and writer, Edwin A. Abbott. It is evidenced in a memoir, disguised as a satirical novel, published in 1894, *Flatland, A Romance of Many Dimensions.* It was published anonymously seven years after its initial writing. It would have been impossible for him to know the process of that major shift in consciousness, almost identical to mine, had he not actually experienced it. It is likely that the purpose of that publication was to acquire feedback to validate his experiences. After receiving critiques, he republished his memoir with a lengthy Preface regarding his errors as well as addressing insights regarding the numerous symbols in that initial writing.[20]

For many years his book was generally ignored. It began to be republished in 1926, the year of his death. It has been republished many times since then. It has been the source of numerous commentaries and the inspiration for numerous books. One of the people he inspired was Claude Bragdon,[21] an architect, validating Bragdon's belief that space is a dimension of the mind. Bragdon also found that validation in the *I Ching.*

Those later publications of *Flatland* contain the subjectivity of its editors, words changed here and there, and Abbott's Preface to his second edition has often been omitted. The reason being that Preface exposes social and psychological issues—an underlying purpose of his writing—to bring positive change to humanity. Even in his initial writing Abbott ends his memoir with the hope that, in some future time, his words "may find their way to the minds of humanity."

Thomas F. Banchoff, professor of mathematics and the geometry of higher dimensions at Brown University, values Abbott's novella as a brilliantly conceived book. He states that Abbott was a theologian and a headmaster of a school in Victorian

England. "As a leader in the movement to provide educational opportunities for young men and women of all social classes, he was often frustrated by establishment views in education and religion. Of his fifty books, the one that still speaks clearly to our own day is his little masterpiece, *Flatland,* simultaneously a social satire and an introduction to the idea of higher dimensions."[22]

Basic to the dimensions in Abbott's novel, Flatland is dominated by the sequential left brain, and Spaceland is reflective of the creative spatial right brain.

Abbott, from early college years had broad interests, not only theology and mathematics, but the classics, especially Shakespeare. In his Preface, he quotes Shakespeare, referring to him as a Spaceland poet: "One touch of Nature makes all worlds akin [makes the whole world kin]." There is a strong possibility that other Spacelanders also served to provoke his awakening. Plato's *Allegory of the Cave*[23] has many similarities to Abbott's experiences described in *Flatland.* 17th century German mathematician and philosopher, Gottfried Wilhelm Liebniz's work regarding spirituality and unclear perceptions [the unconscious], is also implicated in Abbott's book.

In his revealing Preface, Abbott speaks of dimensions beyond Spaceland. He argues that dimension implies direction and measurement and when we go beyond direction and measurement, we cannot know what to measure or in what direction. Yet he believes it to be there. He is speaking of the life force, which manifests in the human spirit, when he says, "Even I cannot comprehend it, nor realize it by the sense of sight or by any process of reason; I can but apprehend it by faith."

Abbott also elucidates his thoughts on patriarchal hierarchy, "those who maintain superiority over multitude of their countrymen by their intellectual power are in conflict with nature; nature in sentencing them to infecundity [lack of creativity] has condemned them to ultimate failure." He also states, "I see a fulfillment of the great law of all worlds, that while the wisdom of man thinks it is working one thing, the wisdom of nature constrains it to work another and quite a different and far better thing."

He dedicates his book to the inhabitants of space in general [those insightful and spiritual people] "so the citizens of that celestial region may aspire yet higher and higher to the secrets of four, five, or even six dimensions thereby contributing to the imagination and the possible development of that most rare and excellent gift of modesty among the superior races of solid humanity."

Abbott's Preface continues in order to acknowledge two major errors in his book, in response to those critiques—one of an intellectual nature, the other one moral—and addresses the corrections. The intellectual two dimensional concept of flatland is actually three. He reports that during the years of contemplating his experiences, the immoral sexist implications toward women and irregulars changed.

Taken as a whole, his use of the words, on the one hand and on the other hand, indicates that he is dealing with conflict between his two hemispheres. The seven years of imprisonment [enmeshment/entrapment] in Flatland, was spent attempting to overcome the impediments to unity and equality.

Abbott's claim to have written Flatland as a historian is congruent with his two dimensional concept of Flatland, for history is available in the educational system in the two dimensional world of books. Those books, in leaving out the dark side of human history, essentially become lies. While he uses geometry to represent the numerous social dimensions of the sequential measurement of human worth, he demonstrates extreme focus on details, which makes it difficult to see the big picture. It is an example of an old saying—one cannot see the forest for the trees.

Abbott divides his novel into two parts, *This World* and *Other Worlds.*

This World In Part One, Abbott's protagonist, a Square, begins his romance by projecting the setting forward more than a century in time to the new millennium—the last day of the year 1999. Millenarianism has two meanings: belief in the millennium of Christian prophecy and belief in a coming ideal society and especially one created by a revolutionary action.[24] Revolution is also addressed in Abbott's Preface.

The Square proceeds to initiate the reader into This World and the inhabitants—geometric figures—and the strictly divided castes of Flatland society. Those social groups are determined by the number and size of the inhabitants' angles.

Circles are the most esteemed of castes, the high priests of the various subjects in Flatland. They have so many angles they diffuse into a curved line. The graduated decreasing angles of even-sided figures, e.g., octagon, hexagon, subdivide the higher castes. The Square is of the professional or gentleman caste. The isosceles triangle represents soldiers and workmen.

In Flatland it is the circles who dictate conformity: irregulars, those with uneven sides and shapes are of the lowest class of males. They are gotten rid of or imprisoned or assigned to some menial, meaningless task. Anyone in Flatland who entertains the notion of dimensions higher than This World is also eliminated or imprisoned.

Women are straight lines; they are the lowest and most pitiable caste, having no angles or any hope of bettering their positions. They are disparaged for being pointed, likened to soldiers, whose sharpness is considered dangerous to other inhabitants of Flatland.

Due to their needling, they are forced to announce themselves with the peace [appease] cry. Their seductiveness is painstakingly described. Their eyes and mouths are perceived as identical, and they evidence no memory, according to the Square, which seems to be a wise pre-arrangement in order for them to cope with their miserable state. Their miseries and humiliation are believed to be a result of natural laws or the product of evolution—that biological determinist view.

In Flatland, evolution to a higher status is usually accomplished by males with even sides. The irregulars, like women, are considered predestined to hopelessness.

The ambient condition in Flatland is primary darkness, exacerbated by the fog, which the Square describes as comforting and necessary to the maintenance of the caste structure of society. The fog [of prejudice] diminishes sensate existence.

In the lower classes, including women, feeling is the only means of recognition. The Square, like others of the professional caste, acquired, through his education, a keen sense of hearing and sight-recognition to determine the illuminated shapes of other inhabitants of This World. Were it not for the fog all would appear equal.

The Square recounts a brief time in history [the Renaissance] when decorative color was introduced, the art that equalized all classes. Art created such havoc that the repressive circles forbade and punished the use of color in the lower castes and reserved it for themselves.

Other Worlds After familiarizing the reader to life in This World, the Square, in Part Two, narrates his introduction to Other Worlds, dimensions that lie both beneath and above the limited environment of Flatland. In his movement toward enlightenment, the Square encounters the revealing world of dreams, ideas, along with the vicissitudes that accompany contradictions to his familiar existence.

In his first dream of dimensions other than This World, the Square is introduced to Lineland where the populace consists of lines and points moving in a single direction, and each can only see the point immediately in front of or behind it. Women are the points, and the lines are males with two different voices on either end, used to attract two wives, each of whom has a voice that harmonizes with one end of the line or the other.

Lineland is obviously an underlying dimension of Flatland—that creation of women as the second sex to pleasure men and to procreate. It continues to be the source of prejudice against women. That dream was the beginning of his creative illness and preceded his awakening.

Another disturbance is the question his grandson asks during his math lesson with the Square on that projected last day of 1999, the query of a child unencumbered by the rigid societal structure of Flatland. The question—a matter of thought progression—if one can square a figure, then what would happen if one cubed a figure and raised the power and the structure to another dimension? The Square, firmly enmeshed in the belief system of Flatland and aware of the inevitable punishment for even thinking of a higher dimension, is shocked; he duly reprimands his grandson.

On that proposed eve of the new millennium, the Square, in ruminating about the year just passing, including his grandson's question, says aloud, "the boy is a fool." He then feels a disconcerting presence, and a voice comes, as if from nowhere, saying that the child is correct. He then experiences a vision of a circle which transforms into a sphere, the character assigned to his spatial brain. The circle, though, arouses fear and the forbidden emotion of anger toward the high priests of each subject dominating This World. It was that unconscious anger which had been subdued to his sense of frustration. Then the Sphere addresses the eye inside—insight. His spatial brain had taken charge. The Square describes his initial experience of space:

> "An unspeakable horror seized me. There was a darkness; then a dizzy, sickening sensation of sight that was not like seeing; I saw a Line that was no Line; Space that was not Space: I was myself, and not myself. When I could find voice, I shrieked aloud in agony: "Either this is madness or it is Hell.""

The voice comes again, "It is neither, it is knowledge." As he slowly adapts to that vision of the character of his spatial brain, the Square is seized by a religious experience and perceives the Sphere as god. It takes some time before he realizes the Sphere is not a god; then the insight that he can only adjust to change by degrees. Another insight—as the illusions of his life began to topple—the shallowness of Flatland and his former blindness.

The square feels empowered by that new-found capacity to see; then the Sphere's voice, "Does this omnividence make you more just, more merciful, less selfish, more loving?" To which the Square replies in shock, "more merciful, more loving, but these are the qualities of women." His spatial brain's question arouses the insight that the wisest think more of humane values and authentic feelings than of understanding, more of the despised Straight Lines than of the esteemed Circles.

Subsequent to the Square's acceptance of the higher dimension that had been rendered unconscious, he becomes exhilarated with thought progression, an arrogance that sends him back to Flatland. That return evokes another dream in which he encounters the lowest depth of existence—the nonmoving, non-dimensional, "vile and ignorant" land of the Point. The single inhabitant of the land of the Point is completely self-contained, self-satisfied, and oblivious of any dimension other than his own; he attributes all existence to his own thought, unable to see, to hear, to move, or to change. In his dream, the Square is astounded at such complacency and, try as he might, he is unable to budge him. His spatial brain stops the futile efforts with the words: "There is nothing that you or I can do to rescue him from his self-satisfaction."

That dream is a major point of Abbott's book. It is complacency that maintains the shallow, oppressive, and spiritless human world dominated by the sequential (left brain) dimension of Flatland.

Convincing fellow Flatlanders of what he learned of Other Worlds is another dilemma for the Square. His efforts to enlighten fellow Flatlanders, even his grandson, serve only to make him an outcast. There was no one in Flatland to validate his memories, his dreams, and his experiences.

Within Abbott's writing are his discoveries of spatial brain attributes much higher than imagination: valid emotions, creativity, humane values, and the capacity to see the big picture—that holistic view. Another major discovery was that it is insight which serves to evolve consciousness. That, together with the human spirit, over time, can take one to the highest levels—that celestial region of the mind.

Disguising his experiences as a novel was, in itself, creative; it is likely that novelty was used in order to resist admitting to the sensation of insanity when his spatial brain took charge. That satirical aspect may have been evoked by the biblical implication that laughter is the best medicine.

Abbott's personal transformation, evidenced in his Preface, resulted in another pertinent article, written years later, also published anonymously: *The Gospels* in the ninth edition of the Encyclopedia Britannica, embodying a critical view which caused considerable stir in the English Theological world.

▲　▲　▲

This author can fulfill Abbott's hope that his work, taken as a whole, reveals the uniqueness of every individual, validating his unique experiences, fulfilling, as well, his hope that in some future time, his words may find their way to the minds of humanity.

Abbott's memoir, written over a century ago, validates the truth of ancient Egypt's empowered humans as well as the impediments to consciousness imposed by that shift to patriarchy. The subsequent mythical god, created in man's image, has furthered the deterioration of human society by the big divide between the right and left hemispheres of the human brain, by oppression of the spatial brain's attributes, rendering them unconscious, especially the human spirit. That big divide is comparable to Jesus' saying in *The Gnostic Gospel of Thomas,* "… I say if one is whole, one will be filled with light, but if one is divided, one will be filled with darkness. The human spirit, the source of that light, also becomes oppressed.

Abbott's Flatland also validates the contents of *The Sacred Canopy,*[25] written by Sociologist Peter L. Berger. In his book Berger asserts that religion serves to legitimize social, economic, political, and cultural traditions of a society. That is true regarding the initial conception of religion; the traditions imposed by the Egyptian shift to patriarchy became evident in Moses' writings.

Moving forward in time, it evolved into Social Constructionism, a term associated with Berger. It is "a school of thought pertaining to the way social phenomena are created, institutionalized, and made into tradition by humans."[26] Berger also knew that religion has wormed its way into every nook and cranny of human society, especially that school of thought. Abbott's description of women's shortcomings in Flatland is also a validation of Berger's assertion that religion has resulted in a woman's tendency toward non-sexual masochism—tolerance of abuse and oppression.

Both Abbott and Berger confirm Stephen Jay Gould's work regarding the double fallacy of biological determinism. Abbott confirms more of Gould's insights: humans are inextricably part of nature; human uniqueness resides primarily in our brains; the dominance of the fog of prejudice resulting in the mismeasure of humans is still evident in the current flatland field of psychology as well as society at large.

Abbott's book does, unfortunately, speak clearly to our own day regarding Darwinian inequities, which continue to contribute to our predominantly patriarchal and materialistic sequential left-brain world. It is also evidenced by the contributors to Daniel C. Maguire and Sa' Diyya Shaikh's revealing book, *Violence Against Women in Contemporary World Religions*[27] in the 21st century.

Another man, anthropologist and physician Dr. Paul Farmer, confronts all of those inequities in his book, *Pathologies of Power: Health, Human Rights, and the New War on the Poor.*[28] It is an eye-opening book and provides numerous examples of the pathologies of the use of power in high places resulting in structural violence—the way by which social arrangements are constructed to put specific members of a population in harm's way. He is fully aware of the effect of materialism in countries where many perish from lack of basic human needs, even food and water.

Dr. Farmer is the founder of *Partners in Health,* which began with his humanitarian work in Haiti and now extends throughout the world. He is a man who has truly made a difference in the lives of countless people. Paul Farmer is dedicated to the philosophy that "the only real nation is humanity."[29]

Although Farmer, like Abbott, is still connected with religion, he is aware of the inequities, that evil oppression, existing within that patriarchal system. His awareness is evident in his support of Liberation Theology, a movement initiated during the 1950s in South America by Catholic priests whose focus was on the suffering of the poor and disenfranchised, even women, and an attempt to evolve Christianity to include humanitarian ideals.

It was a movement, though, that was thwarted by the Vatican that condemned it as being Marxist; the same Vatican that provided escape routes for Nazi war criminals who committed monstrous crimes against humanity. Those inequities have essentially moved the U. S. backward in time with the election of psychopath Donald Trump, comparable to Adolph Hitler, as President.

2

Self-actualization, Modern Sages, and The Multidimensional Reflective Human

Humanist psychologist Abraham Harold Maslow was a victim of the fog of prejudice in his early years, for his parents were first generation Jewish immigrants from Russia. He experienced Anti-Semitism from his teachers and from other children in his neighborhood in Brooklyn, New York. Anti-Semitic gang members even attacked him physically. His home was also a source of oppression due to his mother. Without friends, he essentially grew up in libraries and among books, developing a love for books and learning. It becomes obvious that his early life experiences played a major role in his hierarchy of human needs: physiological, safety, social, esteem, and self-actualization.

It is also obvious that another need should be added—intellectual. The capacity to learn, think, and to question everything in order to achieve experiential knowledge, helped him to overcome the deficiency of safety needs as well as the social need for love and affection.

Maslow's hierarchy of human needs and human values were only the beginning of his contribution to the field of psychology.

Through his own peak experiences—insights—he moved on, through evolution of consciousness, to Holism. While all functioning humans use both brains, it is insight, "the capacity to discern the true nature of a situation; penetration,"[30] which evolves consciousness.

While Maslow lacked knowledge of spatial and sequential brain functioning, it is obvious that his B [humane] values emanate from the spatial right brain, and D [deficiency] values regarding human needs, are sequential left brain challenges. His next move was to transpersonal psychology and self-transcendence—that celestial region of the mind, to borrow Abbott's term. It is congruent with the heaven inside, referred to by Jesus in the *Gospel of Thomas*, reflective of the heaven outside in the harmony of nature—the spirit—the ascending force in both nature and humans.

Maslow's enlightenment and self-actualization was and is a major contribution to the revolution of psychology, especially his top-down view, like those revolutionary Chaos scientists, as well as his innate right brain capacity to see patterns across different scales at the same time. Maslow made quantum leaps in his theories. Like those scientists, his accomplishments were derided. He was accused of lacking science in his conclusions. He was also disparaged by the sequential right wing conservatives, especially Christina Hoff Sommers, social critic, and Sally Satel, a truly psychopathic practicing psychiatrist, who says that Maslow's ideas are no longer taken seriously in the world of academic psychology. Unfortunately, that is true; in my education he was only mentioned in connection with Humanist psychologist Carl Rogers, among the founding members of client centered psychotherapy.

Both Sommers and Satel exemplify the shallow thought processes of the high priests of Flatland circles. They are rational and convincing—egoists in the first degree. They were the authors of *One Nation Under Therapy: How the Helping Culture is Eroding Self-reliance*,[31] a prime example of the two dimensional world of books that dominated Flatland as well as our current educational systems. A commentary regarding that book is that "it is the consequence of their attacks on the human-potential movement, a mid-20th-century offspring of the psychologists Abraham Maslow and Carl Rogers and the parent, in turn, of the self-esteem craze... This school of thought posits the existence inside each of us of an ideal self, 'buried under a lot of wreckage put there by a judgmental, emotionally withholding, unforgiving, and oppressive society.' In this reading, persons we might once have considered sinners or wrongdoers are instead reconceived as the victims of malign social forces, and entitled as such to our empathy and compassion and, frequently, our tax dollars."[32]

Maslow's top-down view of mental health is in contrast to the focus on mental illness. He based his work on people who evidenced self-actualization: Albert Einstein, Dr. Albert Schweitzer, anthropologist Ruth Benedict, Gestalt psychologist Max Wertheimer, Henry David Thoreau, poet, philosopher, naturalist, and abolitionist, as well as Lao Tzu, an ancient Chinese philosopher and writer who was greatly influenced by the *I Ching*.

All of his examples of self-actualized people were aware of reality, in contrast to those who distort the world to fit with their beliefs. They were, as well, aware of the human connection with nature. They, like Maslow, evidenced differentiation and individuation, terms used by Systems Theorist and Psychiatrist Murray Bowen, also ignored in my education. Bowen used degrees of differentiation as a measure of mental health in order to achieve individuation from one's family.

Broadly, *individuation* is the process of becoming a separate individual, using one's capacity to think, feel, speak, and act on one's own—the movement away from mental dependence. While Bowen's concept has validity, he does not address the source of that mental dependence—enmeshment. It is a major impediment to wholeness and balance. It is a concept I discovered in my process of enlightenment.

Enmeshment is the persuasive brain-washing by which the person in the position of authority—whether it be a parent, companion, teacher, theorist, therapist, president, priest, preacher, guru, pandit, gang leader, Ron Hubbard, Adolf Hitler, or Osama bin Laden, in order to gain power and control over other people. Patriarchal religions, founded in animalistic sex and aggression, have always been about power and control. In Christianity, control is accomplished by the threat of hell and the carrot of heavenly reward.

Need is a prerequisite for vulnerability to enmeshment. That need may be a basic physiological necessity or safety needs; it may be an esteem need, social need, need for a sense of purpose. It is a given that all children are vulnerable.

Another part of the enmeshment process is punishment and reward—the promise of need fulfillment to maintain focus. Punishment plays on the fears of people; intimidation, both subtle and obvious, is also a part of that scheme.

The most effective strategy, though, is isolation. That isolation is accomplished by condemning or scapegoating people who threaten the agenda or beliefs of those in position of power, thereby thwarting any dissenting voice. It is a well-known fact that condemnation—the root of hatred and prejudice—is taught. One becomes mentally, and sometimes physically isolated from those who have a different point of view. Isolation is a significant symptom that coercion is taking place.

Murray Bowen's *individuation* is applicable regarding scaling systems. Not only must one abstract one's self from enmeshment in the family, but from human systems at large, especially from religion and the sick field of psychology, which permeates all dimensions of human societies, including politics.

▲ ▲ ▲

As said in the Introduction, regarding the field of psychology: it is most unfortunate that the function of the human brain has been ignored, especially the total disregard of Nobel laureate, neuropsychologist, and neurobiologist Roger Wolcott Sperry's achievements.

Sperry, together with two colleagues, received the 1981 Nobel Prize in Physiology and Medicine for divided brain experiments. Those experiments were done with people whose corpus callosum, the thick band of nerve fibers connecting the two hemispheres, had been surgically severed to control severe epileptic seizures. Those studies resulted in conclusive evidence of the lateralization of the human brain. As said previously regarding the ancient Egyptians' knowledge, the right hemisphere controls the left side of the body, and the left hemisphere controls the right side of the body.

That work was only one dimension of his discoveries, for he was interested in everything from the cosmos to the finite workings of the amazing human brain. That interest began in childhood; he spent his early years on a farm where he developed a lifelong interest in nature. Theodore J. Voneida, a neurobiology educator, both colleague and friend of Sperry, offers Sperry's biology, including his accomplishments, in *A Biographical Memoir*. He concludes that biography with, "Scientist, teacher, philosopher, humanist—Roger Sperry has left us a rich legacy of ideas and a challenge to foster the emergence of new understandings of human capabilities and responsibilities." [33]

It is evident that Sperry, too, was self-actualized—a whole and balanced man. According to Voneida: "Sperry was a quiet, thoughtful, and modest man with an insatiable curiosity. He never stopped working, questioning, or learning up until his death in 1994 of ALS or Lou Gehrig's disease. You could often find Sperry in his office with his feet propped up on his desk scribbling in his notebook or deep in thought. Sperry was an avid paleontologist and displayed his large fossil collection in his home. He was also a very talented sculptor, artist, and ceramicist. He enjoyed going on camping and fishing trips with his wife and children in Baja, California."[34]

Sperry knew that the left brain is superior in analytical, sequential, and linguistics; the right brain performs better in holistic, parallel, and spatial abilities. His comprehension evolved to conclude that the brain is:

"Indeed a conscious system in its own right, perceiving, thinking, remembering, reasoning, willing, and emoting, all at a characteristically human level. . . . Both the left and the right hemisphere may be conscious simultaneously in different, even in mutually conflicting, mental experiences that run along in parallel."

He also reports that "The split brain behaves in many respects like two separate brains, providing new research possibilities."

Those *mutually conflicting* mental experiences, referred to by Sperry, are indicative of the *unconscious,* the spatial brain knowledge which one knows but does not know one knows. Sperry's work also gives credence to instincts hard-wired in the brain as well as the discovery of neuroplasticity. It was once believed the human brain is fully developed by age six; later, that development was extended to age ten. Now it is known that the brain can change throughout life through multidimensional experiences. Current research reveals that experience actually changes the brain's physical structure and functional organization.[35] Neuroscientists have also explained many mysteries such as out-of-body and near-death experiences.[36]

Yet not all neuroscience is valid, like those who are the source of controversy over right and left brain functioning. They base their conclusions on electronic imaging of neuron activity, denying the fact of suppression of spatial brain knowledge—the unconscious. As Stephen Jay Gould knew, through his science historian specialty, many so-called sciences are contaminated by the subjectivity of its researchers. Even theoretical physicists evidence subjectivity, especially in the hypothetical parallel universe, akin to the supernatural. Obviously they lack consciousness of their own parallel dimension (spatial brain) and perceive it outside themselves.

Sperry's work continued to progress. In *Holding Course Amid Shifting Paradigms,* Sperry proposes a shift from scientific materialism to mentalism; a shift from the reductionism of the human to the atomic level to comprehending that the whole is more than the sum of its parts. His new model "involves an added emphasis on the space-time or pattern factors in causation as opposed to the material, physical factors."[37]

In physics, space-time is an additional continuum, which opens the door to numerous dimensions. The mentalism of which Sperry speaks also explains many mysteries, including synchronicity, which simply means to be in sync with the energy of another living entity. Theodore J. Voneida provides an informed summation regarding Sperry's work within that arena:

> The concept of emergence, according to Sperry, "occurs whenever the interaction between 2 or more entities, be they sub particles, atoms or molecules, creates a new entity with new laws and properties formerly nonexistent in the universe." He notes the parallel with quantum physics in which "interactions among subatomic particles result in emergent properties which in no way resemble the particles from which they arose."
>
> Thus, consciousness, in Sperry's view, while generated by and dependent on neural activity, is nonetheless separate from it. Consciousness emerges from the activity of cerebral networks as an independent entity. This newly emerged property which we call "mind" or "consciousness," continually feeds back to the central nervous system, resulting in a highly dynamic process of emergence, feedback (downward causation), newly emergent states, further feedback, and so forth. Reducing consciousness to its separate components obliterates the emergent phenomenon of "mind" with all its great power and uniqueness.[38]

Obviously Sperry's emergent mind concept is the process of evolving consciousness.

In *Holding Course Amid Shifting Paradigms* Sperry quotes himself from previous articles:

"Our new acceptance in science of consciousness and subjectivity, the mental and cognitive, or spiritual does not—as frequently inferred—open the door of science to the supernatural, the mystical, the paranormal, the occult, otherworldly—nor, in short, to any form of unembodied mind or spirit. The strength and promise of the new macro mental outlook is in just the opposite, that is, in taking our ultimate guideline beliefs, and resultant social values out of the realm of the supernatural and otherworldly uncertainties and grounding them in a more realistic realm of knowledge and truth, consistent with science and empiric verification."

He continued by elevating his concepts from the individual to the global level, stating that:

"The new paradigm affirms that the world we live in is driven not solely by mindless physical forces but, more crucially, by subjective human values. Human values become the underlying key to world change."

Sperry brought conclusion to that writing:

"Humanity's creator thus becomes the vast interwoven fabric of all evolving nature. The creative forces and creation itself become inextricably interfused, making it immoral, even sacrilegious, to degrade earthly existence or to treat it merely as a way station."

Sperry's multidimensional concepts are congruent with the wisdom of the ancient sages and other modern sages aware of the wisdom of nature. The human spirit manifests in many ways, especially humane values. Underlying that manifestation is reverence for life as well as fortitude—the "strength of mind that enables a person to encounter danger or bear pain or adversity with courage,"[39]

Sperry has, indeed, left a rich legacy for humanity.

▲　▲　▲

Another whole and balanced self-actualized man is Stephen Hawking, theoretical physicist, cosmologist, and teacher, famous for his TV shows offering knowledge to humanity. While his biography is offered in many ways, none are as pertinent as his telling his own story in the 2013 Documentary, *Hawking*. It is a film which also reflects that wholeness. Fortunate to have been raised in a nurturing environment, he became a lover of life in his youth. Encouraged to become a medical professional, like his father, Hawking believes that he was fortunate to have chosen to pursue his interest in physics, a field in which he can continue to function with a horrendous physical disability. It is likely that his spatial brain did the choosing, unconscious knowledge that something was amiss. One of the attributes of the spatial brain is inner body awareness, in parallel with the sequential brain's outer body awareness.

Hawking's diagnosis of ALS disease with expectation of only a few years of life, over a half century ago, did indeed require fortitude. Through love for his wife and through music, specifically the work of Wilhelm Richard Wagner, he coped with his illness and exhibited the spirit in his reverence for life to use whatever time he had to fulfill his potential.

In a 2012 mini-series documentary, *Stephen Hawking's Grand Design,* Hawking introduces himself as a "physicist, cosmologist, and something of a dreamer. Although I cannot move and have to speak through a computer, in my mind, I am free." Free from any human constructionism—more in balance with the harmony of nature. That introduction was exactly the same in the 2011 documentary, *Did God Create the Universe?* The answer he finds is consistent with Einstein's words regarding that insane personification of nature's energy:

> "I cannot imagine a God who rewards and punishes the objects of his creation, whose purposes are modeled after our own—a God, in short, who is but a reflection of human frailty. Neither can I believe that the individual survives the death of his body, although feeble souls harbor such thoughts through fear or ridiculous egotism."[40]

Hawking's findings also provides relief as evidenced in his words: "For centuries it was believed that disabled people like me were living under a curse inflicted by god. Well I suppose it's possible that I have upset someone up there, I prefer to believe it can be explained another way, by the laws of nature." His statement is confirmed by this author's knowledge that the universe is both accidental and orderly, stars fall as do meteorites; the sun shines on everyone, not a chosen few. Tragic events occur to both good and bad people. It is consistent with the fact that change, both bitter and sweet, is a part of living.

The content of Hawking's two documentaries are inextricably intertwined, each coming from a different direction. In the *Grand Design* he takes us back, scientifically, to the very beginning when there was only negative space and energy, the contraction before the big bang. He leads us through the multidimensional process of change resulting in the formation of planet earth by the fixed laws of nature. He takes us to the very rudiments of life that operates on every scale in string theory.

Hawking also addresses a major existential question, "Is there a meaning to life?" His conclusion is that life has the meaning we give it. That answer is compatible with the freedom to be. Much more knowledge is presented—all thick with meaning.

Another significant aspect of the *Grand Design* is Hawking's likening that creative energy to music, not just any music but the sound of vibrating strings. It is the same kind of music that positively affects the human fetus in the womb and promotes growth in plants; in contrast, hard rock music actually kills plants. Hawking perceives everything as physics—the immutable laws—producing the amazing harmonious orchestration of nature. Einstein, like Sperry and Hawking, was aware of the creative forces existing in nature, as well as in humans. He learned to play violin as a boy; over the years he came to believe that Wolfgang Amadeus Mozart's music reflected the harmony of nature. Classical music, does indeed, serve as a standard of excellence, for it has positive effects on most aspects of the multidimensional human.

Hawking also states that our earth is just right for us and quotes Carl Sagan, renowned astronomer, cosmologist, astrophysicist, and author, "We are a way for the universe to know itself." Similar is Leonardo da Vinci's assertion in the 15th century: to know the workings of the human is to know the workings of the universe.[41] Ancient sages knew, as well, that humans have innate capacities resembling heaven and earth—a microcosm.

It is a concept which is given credence in this author's discovery of the multidimensional reflective human, the basis for Wholistic Psychology:

Not only are we capable of self-reflection, but humans are a reflection of nature. We are comprised of our dual brains, our bodies, and the physical energy to function. We have evolved to reflect, and to reflect on the world around us in our spatial capabilities, where time is irrelevant; and in our timely sequential processes—including the past, present, and anticipation of the future. We also have evolved to reflect the world in our bodies consisting of the many properties of biology and physics: chemistry, mechanics of movement, proportion, including the Golden ratio of pi, and genes that determine form. That physiological energy is evidenced in behavior.

Space-time-matter-energy, as in nature, forms a continuum, an essential word in its established meaning: "a continuous extent, succession, or whole, no part of which can be distinguished from neighboring parts except by arbitrary division."[42] Those arbitrary divisions abound in man-made constructs, especially in shamanism, religion, and the belief based field of psychology.

That which serves to unify the multidimensional human is the human spirit—the animating life force—the greatest mystery of all. That energy is ubiquitous and exists on every level of life, from the microcosm to the macrocosm. It has provoked a sense of wonder throughout recorded history to those conscious enough to perceive it. It is likely to have evoked Albert Einstein's words, "A knowledge of the existence of something we cannot penetrate, of the manifestations of the profoundest reason and the most radiant beauty—it is this knowledge and this emotion that constitute the truly religious attitude; in this sense, and in this alone, I am a deeply religious man."[43] Hawking extended that concept when he said that the same spirit—animating life force—exists in everyone.

Ancient sages revered that energy as the Divine One: "To know this One means to know oneself in relation to the cosmic forces, for this One is the ascending force of life in nature and in man."[44]

Albert Schweitzer, medical doctor, theologian, philosopher, and musician also encountered that energy within. Disturbed by what he considered to be the collapse of civilization in early 20th century Europe—the lack of ethics or humanitarian ideals—he ruminated extensively on the question, "What is civilization?" He found no satisfactory answer in religion or philosophy and believed he was in practically unexplored land.

Schweitzer describes an awakening experience while on a boat trip in Africa: The iron door yielded. There flashed upon my mind, unforeseen and unsought, the phrase, Ehrfurcht vor dem Leben—to be in awe of the mystery of life. Schweitzer's phrase has also been interpreted as reverence for life. [45]

Both Albert Einstein and Stephen Hawking, like Roger Wolcott Sperry, are men of wisdom and also address the practical, including the political systems that are in opposition to reverence for life. Einstein was a critic of capitalism and strongly favored socialist policies that are egalitarian, as well as democracy. In a sense he predicted what is currently happening in our capitalistic, non-democratic, so-called land of the free—increased oppression and lack of human rights. Hawking has had much to say regarding the election of Donald Trump, who he refers to as a demagogue, elected by the lowest common denominator. He is concerned that the U.S. is heading in a troubling direction, especially Trump's unwillingness to support correcting ongoing damage to our life sustaining planet.

It was truly tragic that Bernie Sanders, who, like Albert Einstein, is a democratic socialist, did not receive the support to even become nominated for president, nor did anyone listen when he became an advocate for his opponent, Hillary Clinton. It is total proof that materialism dominates our society. That underlying focus on the bottom line is what Toni Morrison terms "the bottomed out mind,"[46] which, frequently, is a description of those who suppress their higher spatial brain attributes.

Unbalanced people have increased this author's support of the greatness of modern sages. I knew, as those ancient Chinese sages did, that *great* is synonymous with what is right and good. Stephen Hawking, Albert Einstein, and Roger Wolcott Sperry are actually immortal due to their accomplishments that will continue to advance human knowledge of the wisdom of nature.

3

Pathological Field of Psychology

THE MODERN BEHAVIORAL so-called science of psychology is dominated, as Sperry said, by an "objective, mechanistic, materialistic, behavioristic, fatalistic, reductionist view of the nature of mind and psyche." Definitely the result of sequential left brain mode of functioning. It is a field of study and practice led by narcissistic people. Of course there are many exceptions, like Abraham Maslow, whose top-down view has been discounted and overridden by the unbalanced people in the field.

Regarding the history of psychology, Ellenberger's recorded research is worth the read.[47] He addresses the theories of Janet, Freud, Jung, and Adler. While familiar with Freud, Jung, and Adler, I had not ever heard of Janet until reading Ellenberger's book in 1993. I also learned that Alfred Adler was the first theorist to deny the existence of the unconscious. It is obvious that the theories of Freud or Jung do not challenge the bias of sequential brain functioning, for their conception of the unconscious is that it exists beneath consciousness, which they concluded was the ego.

Ellenberger's writing evoked an insight: **The ego is simply a set of stories about one's self adopted and believed.** The ego is in contrast with self-esteem, a sense of self-worth that is achieved by respect for one's own life.

Sperry addressed Freud's id as being "full of carnal impulses and a predisposition to Oedipal and other complexes."[48] Jung's shadow is somewhat less threatening, yet he said that children's conscious problems are a result of "the evil within oneself as well as outside."[49] His patriarchal view is obvious in his statement, "But no one can evade the fact, that in taking up a masculine calling, studying, and working in a man's way, woman is doing something not wholly in agreement with, if not directly injurious to, her feminine nature."[50] Jung was initially an admirer of Hitler—comparable to Trump—for his ego centered rhetoric.

Pierre Janet's work is necessary in revolutionizing psychology. He coined the words, *dissociation* and *subconscious,* and the first theorist, over a century ago, to know there is a connection between events in the subject's past and his or her present day symptoms.

His findings, as well, have been ignored, for cognitive psychology—information processing—has become the major therapeutic approach. It is truly a sequential left brain perspective. Albert Ellis, PhD, is also said to have been instrumental in the shift from psychoanalysis in his rational approach, also known as Rational Emotive Therapy. He focused on erroneous beliefs as the basis for personal dysfunction and emotional distress. That shift was also an outgrowth of the rigid behavioral stance that all behaviors are learned and can be unlearned.

The Cognitive position is that emotional and behavioral problems are due to dysfunctional thinking patterns, and the goal—to change those emotions and behaviors—is to change how the client thinks. Like Adler's Individual Psychology, both the rational and cognitive concepts contain the ridiculous egotistic thinking of the theorist or therapist that one can know what is in the mind of another.

A subdivision of Cognitive psychology—evolutionary psychology—is based on Darwin's theory of biological evolution. It is purported to be an attempt to unify psychology. It definitely has nothing to do with evolution of consciousness, for it is a truly shallow and empty Flatland concept revealing that egoists abound in the field. One particularly, Harvard Professor Steven Pinker, a specialist in language and cognition, is alleged to be one of the greatest "thinkers" of our time by fellow Flatlanders.

Pinker's subjective confession as to how his mind works is evident in his book, *How the Mind Works*.[51] He exemplifies many of Sperry's listing of the modern view of the nature of mind and psyche—behavioristic, materialistic, fatalistic, and especially mechanistic. Pinker's mechanistic computational model of the functions of the brain by mind-as-computer representation, is based on genetic programming of human behavior by natural selection. He also purports dreams to simply be screensavers of mechanical minds. His so-called science, in that book, is limited to a treatise on the functions of the human eye, what he terms reverse engineering, to prove why women look better with makeup; other issues include his argument for atheism and the selfish gene, one of the mindless physical forces which Sperry referred to in his emergent mind concept.

Another of Harvard's faculty adheres to genetic trait theories: Martha Stout. Her conclusions, evidenced in her book, *The Paranoia Switch*,[52] are just as ludicrous as Pinker's when she states that even political leanings—conservative or liberal—are partly "born in the blood." Stout relies on data acquired by a 2005 research questionnaire prepared by political scientists. She also relies heavily on the myth that the world is comprised of opposites when she asserts that liberals and conservatives are necessary and a part of nature.

Stephen Jay Gould had a lot to say about statistical so-called scientific research, like those political scientists. In *The Mismeasure of Man* he cited many cases of totally refuted measurements such as the inheritance of intelligence. One of the more infamous to which he refers is an 18th century theory of phrenology, a theory stating that the personality traits of a person can be derived from the shape of the skull. That theory was the product of so-called "rigorous scientific study," confirming "all the common prejudices of comfortable white males—that blacks, women, and poor people occupy their subordinate roles by the harsh dictates of nature."[53]

It is a fact that experimental design can be manipulated to gain the desired result by choosing the factors that would prove a point and omitting the factors that would not. Many of those results comprise the arbitrary divisions that do abound like William Herbert Sheldon's body types and personality.

The first Diagnostic and Statistical Manual, DSM, was published in 1952. It attracted controversy and criticism from countless professionals, many who asserted that it is unscientific and formed by the beliefs of a few powerful psychiatrists. Its initial publication was, and continues to be financially backed by drug companies. Put simply, those powerful psychiatrists and the drug companies are in the helping profession for the money. The DSM does reveal some valid behavioral patterns, yet it is comparable to a book of horoscopes with symptoms applicable to any given person at any given time. Essentially, it identifies the symptoms as the disease; then the overuse of medications, with detrimental side effects, to treat the symptoms. For many years I wondered why psychopath was not in that book of so-called mental disorders. Obvious to me now, the symptoms are a fitting description of those pathological psychiatrists.

Jerome Frank, PhD, M.D. addresses various counseling practices in his book, *Persuasion and Healing*,[54] co-authored with his daughter. Frank suggests that the theories actually do not seem to matter in the therapeutic process. His 20 year endeavor to determine the outcome across a broad spectrum of theoretical models resulted in his conclusion: "It is not the mastery of technique or the belief system of a therapist that accounts for positive change, but rather his or her personal qualities" (the person). He also asserts many therapies are surprisingly similar to rhetoric (persuasion) and hermeneutics (interpretation).

The title of his book, *Persuasion and Healing,* provides a clue to the responses in his study. The words, rhetoric and hermeneutics, cannot be linked with healing. His conclusion is agreeable—the person of the therapist can support positive change. The person of the therapist can also be non-therapeutic, like Fritz Perls, a Gestalt psychologist whose massive ego overrode any humanistic or client centered view. Evidently Frank is wrong regarding beliefs. As is the case with most so-called research, the results are dubious. How can one distinguish if actual healing occurs or the subjects have simply learned the psychobabble and been persuaded to comply with the therapist's rhetoric? Another example of enmeshment. Regarding hermeneutics—anyone who interprets the symbols of another or knows what is in their mind is, like Freud, engaged in projection—assigning to others what is in one's own mind.

Personally offensive are those psychiatrists and psychologists who associate creativity with mental illness. One of those psychiatrists founded Creativity and Madness, a Continuing Education

Course purported to be psychological studies of art and artists, famous creative people from the past. It is the subjective material novels and movies are made of. It is lunacy to believe one can interpret the symbols in an artist's or composer's creative work. In contrast, there is a subculture of psychology that promotes art and music therapy.

If one even began to document the damage imposed by psychiatrists, psychologists, counselors, and psychotherapists with their rhetoric and hermeneutics, it would fill countless volumes, and in fact, it does. Phyllis Chesler's *Women and Madness*[55] was the first one found. It exposes the horrors—labels, hospitalization, over-medication, rape...—imposed on women by sexist therapists and psychiatrists.

There are now, and have been, numerous fads adopted by psychologists. Some of those fads are so mind intrusive they qualify as criminal. The famous case of Sybil with multiple personalities has been proven to be a hoax. *Sybil Exposed: Memory, Lies and Therapy*[56] by Journalist Debbie Nathan, is precise in the title of her commentary, which also addresses the [false] recovered memory debacle. That hoax has also been described as a cult-like entrapment, and in *Remembering Trauma,* as a "disgraceful therapeutic craze."[57] It was a craze that turned into a witch hunt destroying countless lives. What makes it even more evil is that it was a craze that brings into question the innumerable valid cases of sexual abuse tucked away by silence.

Just as dangerous are the therapists afflicted with the ridiculous egotistic belief in reincarnation. They also use persuasive tactics, false interpretation, and the power of suggestion, during hypnotic trance, to achieve past life regression memories. The use of hypnotic trance, in any case, is dangerous, for it increases the power of the psycho-therapist over the mind of another.

Another fad that toys with the mind is Neuro-linguistic pro-gramming, which has nothing to do with neuroscience. Its use—to gain control over a client—is as dangerous as Richard Bandler, one of its founders, a murderer and cocaine trafficker.[58] Similar is the relatively new pop psychology Eye Movement Desensitization Processing that has proven to be about as affective as faith healing, which is even less effective than cognitive therapy.

I was unaware of Conservative Christian Psychologist James Dobson's 1977 book, *Dare to Discipline,* which promotes corporal punishment, until results of his publication reached the media: the suffering and death of children, even infants, at the hands of their caretakers. That Dobson's brutality is lauded and taught is horrifying.

Less dangerous is the fad of Transactional Analysis—an ex-tension of Freudian concepts—with a focus on conscious conver-sations. A book on that subject is *TA Today,*[59] coauthored by Ian Stewart and Christian Psychologist Vann Joines. It includes some mindless concepts: there is no such thing as a victim; the assertion that clients made decisions in infancy, and, as children, planned their whole lives.

Then there is rebirthing, the child within, forgiveness, gurus, inspirational speakers, life coaching, spiritualist (psychic) advi-sors, those whose rhetoric includes their religious beliefs ... The current popularized label seems to be bi-polar disorder—perhaps symbolic of our humanly constructed unbalanced world.

Reforming or transforming the system as a whole is prevent-ed by the system itself—the self-governing, belief-based entity—a closed system. While one might argue that the variety of concepts is reflective of an open system, it is not. Instead it is an indica-tion of psychology's deterioration to entropy—a measure of how disorganized a system is—reflective of our closed human systems at large. Another defining principle of a closed system is the lack of transparency, hiding the malevolent alliances and practices within the system. Just as our predominately sequential world exhibits structural violence, so does psychology. Even though it has a code of ethics that speaks of humane values, many lack humane values in practice.

It is a system that protects the therapists who practice those dangerous fads, condoning, as well, the continual teaching of fads in required Continuing Education courses. It protects the even more dangerous practitioner who uses drugs to conveniently alter the minds of our most vulnerable population—children and the elderly. There are proven humanistic alternatives to the use of drugs, especially with children, e.g. Howard Glasser's *The Nurtured Heart Approach.*[60] That approach, however, does not focus on the child, but on retraining the parents to be compassionate and consistent.

Perhaps by being in bed with the drug companies, through their generous financial support, the American Psychiatric Association and American Medical Association have, as well, obstructed valid research regarding the long term effect of massive doses of inoculations on brain development, the effect of anti-depressants on the unborn fetus, etc., etc., etc.

It is equally important to focus on that which is missing. Despite the distinguished work of Swiss Psychiatrist Elisabeth Kubler-Ross, made accessible in her 1969 book *On Death and Dying,* there are few therapeutic interventions which include grief. Those stages of grief are everywhere: denial, bargaining, anger, sadness; by no means a complete list, but those most obvious. Resolution, the closure attained through the grief process, is when one learns to let go of the past. Not only is grief generally ignored but many interventions discourage grief with the excuse that people get stuck in it. It is an idea that discounts the fact that denial is also a stage of grief and can be readily identified in unbalanced people.

It is not a joke—the use of the term *psycho therapist*—that many practitioners are as unbalanced as the patients they treat, obvious in their subjective confessions. Like the Jewish counselor I had the misfortune of encountering who said, "People do not change." She took pride in having destroyed the life of a university professor with gossip about his extra-marital affairs (with her). Her children, as well, evidenced extreme lack of balance. The Wicca psychologist surprised me with her statement that "Everything is symbols." I was shaken by a cognitive counselor who was untouched by the tragedy of violence in her client's lives; lack of compassion was obvious with her assertion that she was an objective counselor.

A major disappointment was over a Self-Psychology supervisor from whom I sought support for my work and to learn more about advances in dynamic psychology. In a social situation he bragged about having had sex with his client because women are seductive. Then there are those extremists regarding self-esteem who preach self-love—that narcissistic massive ego which sublimates the spatial brain capacity.

There were numerous unpleasant encounters with complacent people working in the field. One was an experience with my psychoanalytic professor in graduate school, one of the comfortable white males referred to by Gould. He is Freudian, Christian, with the accompanying massive ego. One day in the lecture room I asked a question regarding inconsistencies between theorists and methods of treatment; he walked to my chair in the classroom, stood over me with a threatening posture, grimaced face, and attacked me verbally. I sat there as though frozen until I heard a fellow student say, "How can you sit there and let him talk to you like that?"

There was little difference between that professor and a rigid behaviorist psychologist, a so-called expert in psychological testing. During a job interview, my initial encounter with him, his arrogance and meanness, evidenced in hostile closed questions, was dumbfounding. I chose not to pursue any role that would bring me into any further contact. It was not surprising but deeply saddening to learn, a few years later, that his teenage son committed suicide. The sadness was for the depth of despair that youth had suffered.

As said before, a major missing factor is neuroscience, not only the functioning of the human brain, but the effect of violence on that functioning. Just after the beginning of the 21st century, researchers, John Reed, Bruce D. Perry, Andrew Moskowtz, and Jan Connolly contributed to the traumagenic neurodevelopmental model of mental problems, especially psychosis, which is reversible by therapeutic client centered intervention, especially the support for grief to overcome the wounds from the past. Various researchers in New Zealand, Australia, Scandinavia, and Germany viewed that model as the most scientifically rigorous and logically consistent. However, in the U.S., the domination of biological determinists caused disregard of that model, just as Pierre Janet's pioneering work has been ignored.

Another neuroscience fact that is generally ignored in modern psychology, is that every human dreams, whether recalled or not. The only exceptions are those whose parietal lobe, behind the frontal lobes, has been damaged by stroke. The parietal lobe is involved in the integration of spatial and sequential sensory information, essentially bringing synthesis to the information received by both the left and right hemispheres.

The excuse used in discounting dreams is that it is impossible to know, for certain, what dream symbols mean. That is true, for dream symbols have no intrinsic meaning. Like any symbol, they may have multiple levels of meaning privy only to the dreamer.

One can rest assured that if the meaning of a dream is obscured, the message will be presented in a more emphatic form. Sometimes, though, one must wait to discover the true meaning, for dreams can also be intuitive.

An example of an intuitive dream was evidenced by a child. She described a frightening dream of her father becoming a changeling. In reply to my question regarding her fear, she said that she was in no danger but was worried. A week after that dream, her father was placed in a psychiatric hospital. She knew something was different in her father's general patterns of behavior even though she did not comprehend what was happening.

It has been known for many years that infants spend a great deal of their sleep in REM (rapid eye movement), a/k/a dreaming, integrating all the sensory input introduced to them in their new world. Generally, the amount of time spent in REM sleep declines as people grow older.

The dream state occurs during a stage of sleep when one's body and so-called consciousness is out of the way; it is a state involved in learning and memory; it is involved in problem solving. Learning to sleep on it, in reference to decisions and insight, is to be receptive to the spatial brain capacity and counters impulsivity.

In many instances, recalled dream content is presented in visual-spatial metaphorical symbols—like a painting—indicative of the creative potential. The dream state is involved in many forms of creativity; writers dreaming is nothing new. Like drawing, dreams can reveal much that has been rendered unconscious.

Dream content is about the here and now—what is going on in the dreamer's life—including unresolved events from the past that continue to disturb one in the present. They can be about the body and its functions or malfunctions. Dreams can also reveal conflicts that exist in one's own mind, especially regarding authentic emotions—an attempt to bring synthesis to one's self. Put simply, dreams serve to evolve consciousness.

In a sense, that awareness of dream states and evolution of consciousness is addressed by Gottfried Wilhelm Leibniz, a 17th century philosopher and mathematician. A most unusual man, he fully used his capacity to think regarding the continuum of the dual brains, body, and behavior—that space-time-matter-energy—reflective of nature. Leibniz made major contributions to physics and technology, and anticipated notions that surfaced much later in philosophy, probability theory, biology, medicine, geology, psychology, linguistics, and computer science. He wrote works on philosophy, politics, law, ethics, theology, history, and philology. Leibniz's contributions to this vast array of subjects were scattered in various learned journals, in tens of thousands of letters, and in unpublished manuscripts. He wrote in several languages, but primarily in Latin, French, and German. There is no complete gathering of the writings of Leibniz in English.

Leibniz's work had a great impact on the field of psychology. Leibniz thought that there are many small perceptions of which we perceive but of which we are unaware. He believed that by the principle that phenomena found in nature were continuous by default, it was likely that the transition between conscious and unconscious states had intermediary steps. For this to be true, there must also be a portion of the mind of which we are unaware at any given time. His theory regarding consciousness in relation to the principle of continuity can be seen as an early theory regarding stages of sleep. In this way, Leibniz's theory of perception can be viewed as one of many theories leading up to the idea of the unconscious.[61]

Leibniz's phenomenal mental achievements are reflective of both sequential and spatial brain functioning, for he is obviously aware of the intertwining of all subjects, including politics. Leibniz, like Sperry, has been ignored in the current Flatland pathological field of psychology. He can also play a role in revolutionizing that left brain mindset.

4

Wholism VS The Depravity of the Left Brain's Egotistic Dimension

THE TWO HEMISPHERES of the human brain evolved to work together. Sequential brain functioning is, and has been throughout history, necessary to adapt to and function in one's environment; higher spatial brain functioning is necessary to move toward maturity—personal growth and development—as well as creativity and technology—the movement from invention of the wheel, thousands of years ago, through countless inventions bringing on the modern age. The spatial brain plants the seeds of creativity, and the sequential brain brings those creative ideas to fruition. While the capacity to see the big picture—holistic vision—is fundamental to change, the attendance to details is just as important. It is not possible to perceive both at once.

Both hemispheres are used by all functioning people. Linda Kreger Silverman addresses many of the attributes of each hemisphere in her listing of Auditory-Sequential and Visual-Spatial learning, Appendix I. The following goes beyond learning, especially the giftedness she addresses.

Sequential Left Brain	Spatial Right Brain
Verbal orientation and language	Visual orientation and symbolism
Human Needs: physical, safety, social, esteem, and intellectual	Spirituality: fortitude and reverence for life
Subconscious	
Attention to Details	Holistic View
Logical /rational	Intuition—the capacity to discern patterns
Reality	Imagination, Creativity, Technology
Hedonistic values: pleasures of the five senses	Humane values: honesty/sincerity, compassion/kindness, justice/fairness, wisdom
External physical awareness	Internal physical awareness

Capacity to focus

After the imposition of patriarchy and
religion, the sequential left brain accepted
beliefs as facts resulting in:

Belief Orientation   Knowledge

Ego: beliefs about ones' self,
resulting in inflated feelings
of pride in superiority

Learned prejudices

Learned feelings, e.g.,   Authentic emotions
honor thy parents

Full consciousness, the sequential and spatial hemispheres, united
by the human spirit, results in self-actualization, wholeness, and
modesty.

In contrast, beliefs imposed by religion and human constructionism—prejudices—as well as massive egos, override higher spatial brain abilities, rendering them unconscious. Human needs
are often disregarded by materialistic people.

There are, however, many people, like Dr. Paul Farmer, Fred
Rogers, and even Ludwig Van Beethoven, while still somewhat
enmeshed in religion, have not suppressed those spatial brain capabilities—especially humane principles and reverence for life.
Another is Pope Francis who adopted St. Francis of Assisi's name
due to his being in sync with nature. It is reflective of Pope Francis'

respect for our life sustaining planet. A current article in the NY Times, August 2017, reports that two close associates of the Pope accused U.S. Catholic ultraconservatives of making an alliance of hate with evangelical Christians to back President Trump.

Betty Edwards, in her book, *Drawing on the Right Side of the Brain*,[62] presents a brief but clear and informative synopsis of the history of societal prejudice for sequential left brain functioning, and bias against spatial brain processing. She says that "it is a bias, embedded in the language we use, which favors group conformity over individuality, and that idea is expressed even in our political vocabulary."

Edwards says, "The political right [sequential left brain], for instance, admires national power, is conservative, and resists change. Conversely, the political left [spatial right brain] admires individual autonomy and promotes change, even radical change."

That conservative right wing stance is to maintain tradition, including religion. Democrats—the political left—are associated with liberalism. Modern American liberalism is "characterized by social liberalism and combines ideas of civil liberty and equality with support for social justice and a mixed economy. The American modern liberal philosophy strongly endorses public spending on programs such as education, health care, and welfare."[63]

There is, however, a need to bring unity to the Democratic Party, for that liberalism can be excessively diverse. It is reverence for life which can serve as a uniting force, as well as a reformed expression of the Party's purpose: to sublimate the depravity of the Republican Party by supporting human needs, humane values, individual autonomy, and equality, as well as technology to protect our life sustaining planet.

▲ ▲ ▲

Depravity—total lack of respect for life—is also addressed in three Zeitgeist film series. The 2007 *Zeitgeist, The Movie*, Part I, addresses the consistency of myths underlying religions, including Christianity, essentially confirming that myth is a traditional story resulting from phenomena of nature. It addresses pagan myth similar to mythologist and writer, Joseph Campbell's comparative mythology. Part II proposes a right wing conspiracy regarding the 9/11 attack. The interplay of war and monetary gain is proposed in Part III.

The 2008 *Zeitgeist Addendum* generally elaborates the underlying causes of materialism.

In the 2011, *Zeitgeist, Moving Forward* documentary, the connection between violence and mental illness is addressed by Gaber Mate', M.D., one of the spokesmen in that film; he specializes in addictive disorders. His statement, "Blaming genes is a cop-out that allows people to ignore the societal factors that contribute to violence."

Another significant spokesman in that film is James Gilligan, a Psychologist who works with imprisoned people who have committed violent crimes. Gilligan reports that those criminals are victims of incredible violence—victims who become perpetrators. He also states that we "can't understand anything outside its environment."

Richard Wilkinson, a British social epidemiologist and another spokesman is obviously aware of neuroplasticity, for in that documentary he addresses the biological effect of violence. He proposes that it can even activate genes. Yet he does not address the fact that emotional and psychological abuse can be just as damaging.

As said in the Introduction, Stanford neurobiologist Robert Sapolsky also appeared in that film. It is generally known that stress lowers the effect of the immune system and plays a role in physical illness. Sapolsky extends the effect of stress to pre-birth and the human brain, for the womb is the first environment which plays a major role in one's development. Not only is the fetus affected by the foods, drugs, alcohol the mother consumes, according to Sapolsky, stress on the mother imposes stress on the fetus.

Sapolsky, in his 2008 National Geographic Documentary, *Stress: Portrait of a Killer*[64] also takes stress to a scaled up level when he concludes that hierarchical arrangements contribute to stress in everyday life. Patriarchy is the main contributing factor to hierarchical arrangements and social class.

The results of stress were also addressed by Mate' who introduced the terms *explicit* and *implicit* memories. Obviously unaware of the attributes of the sequential and spatial hemispheres, he asserts that implicit memories sustain addiction—those authentic emotions that have been rendered unconscious. Another example he presents regards adopted infants who felt the pain of being taken away from their mothers. Mate' is also aware that without human touch, infants' brains do not develop.

Essentially, the psychological aspect of that film gives credence to the sequential hemisphere-spatial hemisphere-body-behavior continuum; damage to any dimension affects the others.

Structural violence was also a focus in *Zeitgeist, Moving Forward;* numerous examples were given linking that violence to the profiteers—the product of social constructionism—the materialism that has taken over much of the human world. A world where even illness, physical and mental, is advanced for profit.

The solution to resolve the problems of our shallow and violent world contained a concept that is most agreeable, the need for a revolution and a restructuring of society more in tune with nature, one founded in a resource-based economy. It would dissipate the inherent depravity in capitalism, which fosters economic inequality, and replacing it with a social system that meets changeless human needs.

Jacque Fresco, another spokesman in that documentary, evidences no wisdom at all in his Venus Project, in which no one has to work; it is not only absurd but totally out of balance with nature. Frescos' obsession with that project is indicative of his subjectivity. It is evidenced in the fact that he was not ever successful in his jobs or human relationships, even in his family.

Subjectivity includes one's personal taste/perception, opinions, as well as one's subconscious. Subconscious is "that part of the mind which is on the fringe of consciousness and contains material of which it is possible to become aware by redirecting attention."[65] The subconscious is essentially one's history, including events from the past available for recall when attention is drawn to them.

The subconscious is the source of mild mental dysfunctions—neuroses—caused by stress imposed by abuse. Anxiety, depression, and obsessive behavior are prime examples. Obsessive behaviors, evidenced in alcoholics, workaholics . . . serve to maintain dissociation from one's subconscious.

The more severe mental dysfunction—psychosis—as said before regarding the traumagenic neurodevelopmental model, is caused by chronic abuse. The symptoms, characterized by defective or lost contact with reality, is the result of the major functions of the sequential brain rendered unconscious by overwhelming fear and a total lack of a sense of self-worth. The so-called hallucinations reflect the lack of sequential language development, replaced by symbolic language, both visual and auditory, like a dream. The drugs used to treat those symptoms are powerful anti-anxiety medications, which can cause permanent damage to both the mind and body.

Raising the Level of Sequential Left Brain Oriented Educational Systems

Just as religion must be removed from politics in order to reform human systems, it needs to be removed from educational systems, from kindergarten through high school. It can be replaced with self-knowledge, respect for life, and the sciences of nature, including evolution.

Stephen Hawking is a master teacher, evidenced in his film series, *Genius*. He chooses ordinary people and encourages them to ask all the questions in their mind. He also challenges them to learn to answer their own questions by creative problem solving.

Creativity and imagination need as much emphasis in lower educational systems as the basics of math and language. There are teachers in many schools who know that courses in art are especially important. As Betty Edwards says, drawings "reveal much about you to yourself, some facets of you that are obscured by your verbal self."[66] Drawing, though, can, over time, actually change one's language when the artist gains insight regarding his/her work—the movement toward self-knowledge. Unfortunately, schools in poor neighborhoods are lacking that emphasis and definitely need to be upgraded to further equality.

Another subject in those degraded schools that need emphasis is music, especially training in playing musical instruments. That skill actually changes the brain; it is said to "accelerate cortical organization in attention skill, anxiety management and emotional control."[67] *Music of the Heart* is a 1999 movie based on the true life story of Roberta Guaspan, who, through love and persistence, positively affected the lives of thousands of children and families with her teaching of Harlem ghetto children to play violin. It is a movie which remained in my subconscious mind regarding the valuable lessons that can be learned through music.

Another major spatial brain skill can be accomplished by journaling, for one's thoughts, and especially one's authentic feelings, written on paper, take on reality. Another master teacher is Erin Gruwell who was aware of that fact; her extraordinary accomplishments in the minds of her students can be found in *The Freedom Writers Diary: How a Teacher and 150 Teens Used Writing to Change Themselves and the World Around Them*, by Freedom Writers and Zlata Filipovic. It is the basis for the 2007 movie, *Freedom Writers.* Gruwell's motivation for asking her students to keep diaries was intercepting a racist drawing from one of her students. It is an example of opening one's whole mind which can bring transformation, fulfilling the potential for wholeness.

There is a need for physical education courses to actually produce knowledge of the functions of the human body. While many states require sex education classes, there are just as many that do not. Comprehensive sexual education supports young people to make healthy decisions about sex and to adopt healthy sexual behaviors; the possibility of sexual abuse also needs to be addressed. Moving other physical education subjects away from competitive game playing to learning relaxation and strengthening exercises like Tai Chi and Yoga, could be of lifelong use for healthy functioning.

High school and college required education courses should include Wholistic Psychology regarding the functions of the human mind, especially the potential for wholeness and balance, as well as the impediments produced by human constructionism. That knowledge would increase the possibility of higher functioning people in all fields of work.

Teachers who are cognizant of the effect of abuse on the mind can be more alert to students who are victims and can intervene to rescue them from their oppressive environment. It is not always the parents that impose that abuse; it can be extended family members, siblings, neighbors, priests, preachers, bullies, and even egotistic teachers.

As said before, Jerome Frank, PhD, M.D., in his summation of his book, *Persuasion and Healing*[68] regarding counselling, discovered that it is the *person* of the therapist who can bring positive change. He then asks the question, how can education in the field of psychology aid in training that *person*. The answer is relatively simple, not only being trained in revolutionized psychology, but by required examination of their own lives through introspection, as well as making changes to achieve balance in their own lives.

Wholistic Psychology is the basis for the definition of mental health. While no one is perfect, It is the quality of functioning for which one can strive:

Mental health is balanced wholeness: one's sequential and spatial brains, body, and behavior unified by the human spirit, living separately but together with other people.

The healthy reflect stability, which is rooted in reality and the detailed, sequential side of living as well as the capacity to focus. It is being responsible for one's daily life. With that firm foundation one evidences flexibility to cope with change, both bitter and sweet, which is a part of living.

The healthy reflect insight attained through introspection and engaging the creative spatial brain's capacity to see the big picture—holistic perception—and the ability to discern patterns; engaging, as well, the spatial brain's authentic emotions, inner body awareness, and firm humane principles beginning with the essentials of honesty and sincerity.

Within the process of using all of those natural powers and abilities, one discovers and engages unique talents and the fulfillment of one's potential; discovering as well, one's sense of purpose.

If Wholism creeps into society, it will definitely bring positive change to our systems at large, including our political system, by enhancing Democrats' capacity to override depraved Republicans' resistance to change.

5

Self-knowledge: The Pathway to Wholeness and Freedom

As evidenced in the Gnostic Gospels, knowledge of oneself leads to salvation, synonymous with emancipation. Mahatma Gandhi raised salvation to a universal level in his statement, "You must be the change you wish to see in the world." He knew that change involves engagement with one's inner world.

Even though Dr. Thomas Szasz was fully aware of the sick field of psychiatry/psychology, he also knew that therapy could help patients to acquire self-knowledge. Abraham Maslow's Humanistic Psychology, more like Gnosticism, reveals that people possess the inner resources for growth and healing and that the point of therapy is to help remove obstacles to individuals achieving them.

As said before, the work of Abraham Maslow has essentially been condemned in the field of psychology. Even without knowledge of his findings, I came to the same conclusions in my work as a counselor.

I knew from the time of my earliest internship at a mental health center that every client is unique. Sessions always began with regard for basic human needs, especially safety, by providing clients with a safe place to explore their lives. Over time, physical needs were addressed after discovering that there are physical disorders that affect mental functioning, like hypo and hyper thyroidism, diabetes, and, of course, stress.

After the years of required internship my license was obtained, and I opened a private practice in Maitland, Florida. It was successful through referrals from clients, colleagues, and a psychiatrist who appreciated my insightful work with his patients. That success increased over the years, for it was not only achieved through insight, but through intuition and compassion for my clients. I had stopped labeling any of my clients, for I no longer perceived them as mentally ill, but victims of violence—physical, emotional, and structural—essentially wounded and oppressed.

One of the few tools used in therapy sessions was a genogram, another contribution by Systems theorist Murray Bowen. It is a visual image of one's extended family history. Asking the client to provide descriptions of those people often revealed many dysfunctional familial patterns. It was a visual aid to me as well as the clients to gather their history. It tapped into their subconscious mind. That visual aid frequently brought to the forefront the baggage from the past existing just beneath the surface.

I became more aware of the real value of Bowen's genogram years later when a close friend, younger than me, said, "I owe you my life;" she focused on the time I recommended that visual aid to introspection. Her own personal growth and development has been phenomenal. Similarly, a long-term client, many years later, thanked me for helping her find her life. Most surprising, though, was a client who considered me to be his angel. It becomes apparent to me now that underlying all of my work as a counsellor was unconscious knowledge of the human potential.

I became conscious, though, of the value of writing therapy notes, for, over time, patterns of behaviors, thoughts, and feelings would emerge. My intuitive work progressed; when someone had difficulty expressing themselves or what they were feeling, I began to hand them a piece of paper and asked them to draw. It seemed obvious to me that the HTP psychological test, comprised of drawing a house, a tree, and a person, often revealed subconscious experiences as well as unconscious spatial brain knowledge. Even the simplest drawing, like a dream, can "reveal much about you to yourself, some facets of you that are obscured by your verbal self" to requote Betty Edwards. Her book validated so much of what I knew intuitively.

A drawing by a young woman exemplified that unconscious inner body awareness. It was an image of two overlapping ovals out of alignment. Her head was also slightly tilted. Fortunately, I was able to recognize the source: her atlas, the vertebral connection of the spine to the skull, was subluxated, which, over time, can affect the entire body, even mental clarity and emotional stability. It was confirmed by a chiropractor who corrected the misalignment, overriding the referring psychiatrist's label of major depressive disorder. There were, however, safety, social, and esteem obstacles that were addressed.

▲ ▲ ▲

On January 28, 1990, strange and disturbing visual dreams began to occur. It was the beginning of my creative illness, for on April 1st those dreams began to take verbal form, and I would awaken with poetry in my mind. My awakening, a year later, was the result of a vision recorded in the journal I had been keeping since those strange and disturbing dreams began. The vision:

"I saw a light that began to move and flow in every possible soft color, in dimensions that even defy imagination and certainly any concept I have of space, of direction, of size, or shape. In that vision, the structure of the [humanly constructed] room totally dissipated as did its contents, as though carried by that light; everything seemed to be turning inside out and upside down from what it was and absolutely topsy-turvy to anything rational."

That turning, inside out and upside down, is a form known to exist in physics' string theory. The words produced by that experience: I can see everything!!! It also evoked memories. One scene, apparently indelible in memory: Sitting in the darkness on a grassy knoll, gazing at the night sky, I made a wish on all the stars of the cosmos, please, oh please, let me be all that I can be. That scene occurred on an isolated farm in central Florida when I was 16. Another memory was of my writings as a teenager about a consciousness into which one could tap and a higher plane of existence where one could live. Those writings were destroyed when my mother accused me of being insane.

The elation of my awakening—instantaneous shift in consciousness—dissipated as that *seeing* moved through multiple dimensions, and the illusions of my life began to topple. The first was a change in visual perception, particularly of size. The next was when, in my mind, I saw images of history moving like a film running at high speed—the destruction done in the name of God. Those moving scenes produced a sudden insight: I had not ever been in control of anything, including my own mind.

Consciousness continued to evolve with countless insights— peak experiences, to borrow Maslow's term—as well as my research to try to comprehend what was, and continued to be happening to my mind. In 1993 that research seemed to culminate in a writing regarding the multidimensional reflective human, not only the capacity to self-reflect but a reflection of all of nature.

Now I know that the poems in my journal included the directives of the changes one needs to make to fulfill the capacity for wholeness and balance as well as the highest of human callings—self-actualization. They also included man-made impediments that must be overcome.

Those directives were as follows, together with explanations of their meaning achieved after many years of contemplation and ongoing evolution of consciousness. The following poem is of primary importance, for it has been the source of inspiration for much of my writing:

Heavenly bodies of childhood lose their brightness
with spoiled dreams, books, and close-up photographs;
life becomes but a caricature, like heavenly bodies.

You can take heart if you want to marvel,
one phenomenon grows with each encounter,
the human spirit, greatest mystery of all.

Appreciate complexities of survival,
for no spoiled dreams, books, or close-up photographs
can take away the wonder of that ascending power.

The first words of that poem were based on an interpretation of my first disturbing dream—all children are born innocent, in conflict with the Christian doctrine of original sin, as well as the fact that we are made of the same material as stardust with the inherent brightness of the human spirit. Negative social influence does damage to that innocence with nightmares invoked by fear, as well as books contaminated by the author's subjectivity and human world constructionism. As said before regarding Abbott's two-dimensional books, in leaving out the dark side of human history, they essentially become lies. Those close-up photographs represent the arbitrary divisions of the self by egotistical people who have no concept of the whole.

Life becomes but a caricature when one is enmeshed in human world constructionism. Survival is, indeed, complex, for it includes the countless environmental dimensions that affect one's life in our predominantly violent, shallow, and spiritless left brain society. For many years, perception of the human spirit was seen in others, especially my clients, unaware that their spirit was awakened by my reverence for their lives.

> Give up the ghost of the past;
> do not contemplate confusion.
> Go to the garden to discover
> the art of creation.
>
> One cannot a big tree bend
> nor make flowers bloom;
> only clean one's own debris,
> plant a seed, and
> tend the art of patience.

All change takes time to adjust, especially inner change evoked through introspection as well as creativity. That poem validates Edwin A. Abbott's insight—one can only change by degrees. Much later I learned that those experiential changes actually change the brain's physical structure and functional organization. It definitely takes patience to achieve change that is permanent.

> In my dream appeared a being,
> fascinating concept and unique,
> filled with light, yet fully human.
> No extremes of good or bad,
> not for worship or for hate.

> Time has come for destruction
> of defiled being, the split healed.
> Master plan, conceived by man,
> double-binds the mind, and
> futility darkens the Spirit.

Humanity's evolution from the simplest life form to the multidimensional human, empowered by the light of the spirit, is the phenomenon of being. No extremes of good or bad is the concept of modesty—the moderation achieved when the sequential and spatial brain are united by the spirit. The Master Plan is the evil produced by man seeking control over other people, the basis of organized religion. The double-bind is the process of enmeshment produced by the carrot of heavenly reward and the threat of burning forever in hell. That Master plan results in futility, especially in women, a lack of a sense of self-worth.

Self-esteem can be so low that self-blame can occur for the bad things that happen in one's life. It can even distort perception of one's own body, like the symptoms of anorexia nervosa or bulimia. The split between the sequential and spatial brain does defile one's sense of being. It also suppresses the spirit, the ascending power within, which not only serves to unify one's self but can serve to unify humanity. We are all sisters and brothers of the phenomenal human species.

> Despair one attempts to evade,
> the word that suicide is made of,
> the facing of the truth of evil,
> no chance of reconciliation.

> Children bear the horror,
> the damage goes unseen;
> silent, killing, evil does exist
> in the eyes of complacency.

> Turn the other cheek from the vomit,
> the child cannot stomach the horror;
> call it mental illness, label it if you please,
> death of this society.

"Turn the other cheek," in that poem, is both literal and symbolic. It is a phrase attributed to Jesus in the Christian bible,[69] prefaced by "resist not evil," that is far too often taken literally as is spare the rod and spoil the child. As said repeatedly, complacency is what maintains our violent, shallow, and spiritless, world. Complacent people exhibit mindlessness, like the three monkey syndrome, see no evil, speak of no evil, and hear no evil. Evil is not the opposite of the good, it is the destroyer of the good.

The source of that poem was a client who evidenced the symptom of bulimia. After establishing a working relationship, she began bringing paintings of suffering children to share with me. They were symbolic of those things she knew but could not or had not been able to verbalize. Over time she disclosed the familial brutality experienced throughout her childhood and youth. Bringing that brutality to the surface, she was faced with inevitable grief. After resolving the wounds from her past, her symptoms disappeared; she continued to change through personal growth and development. She is one example of my learning about symbols; they are frequently evident in symptoms, always evident in dreams. They can be displayed in body language and can even be expressed in behaviors.

That poem can also serve as a directive to protest, and/or take action, when one encounters abuse in any dimension of scaling systems—familial, community, state, country, and even global, in order to reform our declining human systems and to resist movement into the silent killing evil of complacency. Witnessed child abuse or neglect or even spousal abuse should always be reported to law enforcers. One can make a difference by contributing to non-profit organizations, like feeding the homeless, supporting the Southern Poverty Law Center which works for justice, and Partners in Health, internationally preventing needless death from illness and even starvation. Calling and writing senators and representatives to protest depraved governmental actions can also make a difference.

> Do not bother with those who do not seek,
> hiding behind the scene of perfection;
> their pointing fingers show
> the wrong direction.

A directive of how to deal with complacent people: those who are self-satisfied and see non-complacent people as the problem.

> Spirit requires a disciplined mind
> with faithfulness of purpose
> for revelation to be complete.
>
> To deviate, mind does forsake
> and calculates to seek,
> with ease, another story.
>
> It looks in another's face
> to find flaws it would hide;
> its own mirror points the finger.
>
> Past is dead one would believe,
> now it is time truth to seek,
> mistakenly without discomfort.

A disciplined mind is one that exhibits fortitude, that strength of mind that enables a person to encounter danger or bear pain or adversity with courage, as well as the capacity to focus. It is similar to Jesus' directive in the *Gospel of Thomas,* "Know what is in front of your face, and what is hidden from you will be disclosed to you." It also takes that discipline to seek the truth of one's own life through introspection. The word mirror, in that poem, was indicative of a major symbol in my poems; the image of a mirror was, as well, in many dreams. It is symbolic of self-reflection, "the capacity of humans to exercise introspection and the willingness to learn more about their fundamental nature, purpose, and essence."[70]

During the process of introspection, one can discover and engage unique talents to move on—through personal growth and development—to self-actualization.

We do not need a world filled with poets, artists, or musicians, especially those who lack the crucial element of insight. There are and have been people in every field—medical, legal, political, philosophical, scientific … even investigative reporters—who have bccome that change and contributed to the benefit of humanity.

▲　▲　▲

The poetry, reflective of what I learned as a counselor, contributed to my own personal growth and development.

My initial poem was personal:

Word aphasia,
even brained,
an oddity.

Countless thoughts
locked inside,
no words could tell.

They tumble out,
and the taste
is bittersweet.

I had learned in graduate school that people with above average intelligence generally exhibit a mental preference for verbal-sequential or visual-spatial functioning as measured by the Wechsler IQ test. Even brained intelligence is an oddity, which happened to apply to me. That word aphasia, though, is indicative of my weakness—auditory language—for recall of words, especially titles and proper nouns are overshadowed by images in my mind. That even brained oddity has been a challenge throughout my life—interested in and curious about EVERYTHING.

In rereading my journal in 1994, as well as unconsciously following those directives, I spent two years writing my biography which, like those strange and disturbing dreams, brought on a storm of emotions. My writing voice, though, was pathetically passive—that verbal weakness I had to overcome. The bittersweet applied to my beloved younger brother, who, over time became an alcoholic and the identified patient of our dysfunctional family. I saw his symptoms as indicative of his being a victim of multidimensional evil. Some of the flaws I saw in him turned out to be my own as well, especially lack of a sense of self-worth. We were both raised by a fundamentalist Christian mother who imposed physical, emotional, and psychological abuse, and a secular, controlling, and bigoted father.

There were no new memories, for many had been recorded in a little diary, one of many previous attempts to examine my life. The major spatial brain awakening was of valid emotions. In retrieving those memories it felt as though I was actually reliving them. The truth of my life was, indeed, a source of discomfort. Now I know that suppression of those emotions was indicative of the complexities of survival. That suppression prevented the movement into psychosis and sublimation of the spirit.

Also included in my biography were the rich events in my former life—due to my even brained oddity—including worldwide travels and resourcefulness; I have often been referred to as a renaissance women.

> Disembodied memories
> paint surrealistic pictures
> to disturb my soul,
> yearning to escape
> unspoken, broken pieces.
>
> Specter from hell,
> taunt me no more
> with bewitching
> intentions of
> unspoken, broken pieces.
>
> Attend your own
> pale countenance
> seeking to dissect
> me to find your
> elusive soul.

A poem evoked by an evil psychologist who, through enmeshment and the false recovered memory fad attempted to destroy my life. I had sought help when those strange and disturbing dreams began. It became evident in my journal—the personal stories he told—that he is a misogynist. At the root of misogyny is that hideous jealousy. He was also the source of my discovery of what enmeshment is. It became evident in his behaviors and words recorded in my journal over a period of eighteen months. He totally disregarded my poetry and art, and criticized anyone who could have been a support to me. It was when he attempted to separate me from communication with my daughter that my spatial brain took charge and rescued me from that entrapment. I confronted his anti-therapeutic behavior; my awakening occurred a week later.

When my spatial brain took charge I experienced a brief, twenty-four hour sensation of insanity. While that psychologist could not stop my process of enlightenment, he became another impediment I had to overcome; my poems were hidden in a closet for over a decade. My experiences with that evil man sparked the necessity of examining the history of the pathological field of psychology. Now I know that even during the nightmare experiences with that psychologist who imposed terror, fortitude was with me, for at no time did I fail to maintain the responsibilities of my daily life, including continual care for my clients. I also became aware of how foolish it is to blindly trust anyone, especially in the fields of psychology and psychiatry.

> Darkened, that face of mine
> with the sleep of death,
> forty years, frozen
> tears did mummify.
>
> Words spoken through the mask,
> tight lips did murmur,
> please release my soul
> to fulfill my task.
>
> An endless line a circle made,
> colored with rich bright rose;
> across its girth a blackened blade
> with a double edge.

It spoke to me of endless love
so rich, pure, and innocent,
it would carve in timeless space
the true strong sign of mother.

Oh sisters, if I could only
tell the beauty of that love
and our painful, giving task,
the true strong sign of mother.

Sever the golden chord you hold,
release your sons and daughters;
they are not for your comfort made
nor for your guilt to carry.

Give them instead the gift of rose
and with the blade across your breast,
endure your own magnificence;
live as their example.

Those frozen tears was a suppression of the grief imposed by my parents. The symbolic vision revealed that true love for my daughter was at the root of my motivation for change.

The mask, in that poem, was a mystery, yet an image of it suddenly appeared in my mind months later; an image I was compelled to draw. Even that drawing was a mystery, evidently evoked by my spatial brain. Its symbolic meaning became evident during those years of introspection and the writing of my biography. It was an image of enmeshment in religion—the raping of the mind.

Severing the golden chord was a directive to free my daughter from enmeshment and to support freedom of choice regarding her own life. Her life has become successful in multiple dimensions, especially supporting fulfillment of human needs and human values.

It was in 1994 that music began to be conceived in my mind; all of my music was dictated by my spatial brain, providing comfort as well as expressing authentic emotions. Some of my compositions, though, like my poetry, took years of contemplation to comprehend the symbolic meaning, for they foreshadowed evolution of consciousness.

The first piano composition was titled *Silk,* a word mentioned in a poem of love. Like most symbols which originate in the unconscious, it is a word that had many meanings for me. The second song was titled *Sacred Marriage,* which I did not understand at the time. It is the whole self, unified by the spirit—the life force—the ascending force in nature and humans. Both of those discarded compositions have recently been retrieved, joined together, orchestrated, and re-titled *Golden Ratio's Stability in Time and Space.* It could just as well be titled *Vitruvian Woman,* for it is a musical rendition of Leonardo Da Vinci's pen and ink drawing of a male in two superimposed positions inscribed in a circle and a square, reflective of the golden ratio, also known as the divine proportion, existing throughout nature. The spirit also unifies humans with the creative forces of nature.

The third song was originally titled my daughter's name. It, too has been retrieved, edited, orchestrated, and renamed *A Mother's Song.*

The fourth song was *Muse of My Music,* another piece evoked by the love poem after loss of the romantic love of my life, my Polish husband, highly cultured in European arts, especially classical music. He was a conservative Catholic; I left him when he became complacent.

Turning the Stone, is the music that helped me to bring my father's death to resolution. Through writing my biography, including the family history, I was beginning to understand that he, like my mother, was a victim of oppression and abuse, and both of them became perpetrators—the evil that is carried from generation to generation.

The first orchestrated composition conceived in my mind came as though it had already been written. It forced me to find a composition teacher, for I did not know how to write all those layers of sounds. I was fortunate to find a kind young man for a teacher. His kindness became a major source of encouragement, and he was more therapeutic than any so-called therapist had ever been. He never criticized, just gently guided, and always exhibited interest in the emotions and events culminating in my music. He described the accomplished piece as a canon and recognized its shape is that of a palindrome: the same backward and forward. It is titled *Reflections on Majdanek,* evoked by a life altering experience at Majdanek, the Nazi death camp memorial bordering the town of Lublin, Poland. That experience also evoked a vow—I will never be silent again.

It was the second vow evoked in Poland. The first was a peak experience initiated by a close encounter with nature—the insight that it is man-made beliefs that impose the borders in one's mind. It was an experience that also validated Plato's *Allegory of the Cave:* the chains that bind the mind are formed by belief and fastened by fear. My vow was to face all of my fears.

Those insights contributed to continued compositions. *Colors of Dawn,* was performed at my second recital at Rollins Community School of Music. It was my first attempt to produce a musical rendition of that awakening vision. Its form essentially suggests that the human spirit is the fifth dimension of the Self, even though it is revealed in the spatial hemisphere. Another piece, *Relative Time,* expressed the positive encounters with people in my life, no matter how brief, that contributed to my knowledge, including many of my clients.

In 1997 a song titled *Colors* was written. *Colors* also became the title of my music album. It represents the passions that bring color and meaning to one's life. It was inspired during the time I was working as a group counselor at the Center for Drug Free Living in Orlando, Florida. My passion was to promote personal growth and development of the members of the group, as well as healing their wounds from the past. The tactics used were introspection, art, and free expression of thoughts and feelings in a journal that was kept private. By then I had realized the importance of self-expression through journaling. Journals often reveal patterns of one's own thoughts, emotions, and behaviors—self-knowledge—as well as the need for self-correction. There were no relapses by members of the group.

One of those clients gave me a precious gift on August 6, 1997, *Life's Little Treasure Book ON WISDOM,*[71] inscribed with a personal note—Dear Frances: I hope that life gives back to you what you so generously give away. Thank you for everything.

A Winter's Night is a song that helped me through grief over my brother's suicide in 1998. It too, needs to be orchestrated and re-titled *The Bitter and the Sweet,* which is a part of living.

The last piece written during my composition education was a string quartet titled *Death of Narcissus,* an ancient metaphor symbolic of words of wisdom: self-love—that narcissistic left brain ego—must die in order for humanity to flower.

In 1996, I also began to fulfill another creative potential—approaching a plain white canvas and allowing my spatial brain to take charge. It was a directive implicated in Betty Edward's book *Drawing on the Right Side of the Brain.* My paintings, like my music, were symbolic of thoughts that would eventually become conscious.

June, 1999, I made a major move to Tallahassee where my daughter and grandson lived. It was more than just a physical move; in a sense I was moving back into the human world. With the exception of part-time employment, most of the previous six years was spent in solitude. It was necessary in order to examine my life, fulfill creative tasks, as well as continuing to overcome the impediments to wholeness and balance. Being a woman in a predominately patriarchal world raised those impediments exponentially. Now I know that the choice to be alone included individuation; as said before, it is a process of becoming a separate individual, using one's capacity to think, feel, speak, and act on one's own.

After the move, my musical creative work continued but at a much slower pace, for I could not find another composition teacher; many are prejudiced against a woman's capacity to compose classical music. Eventually two more songs were written, *A Song of Life* and *Embrace the Mystery*. *A Song of Life* is a musical rendition of Henry Wadsworth Longfellow's poem, *A Psalm of Life.*(Appendix II) That music evoked consciousness of the effect that poem had on my life, even the similarity of the form of his poem with my own. *Embrace the Mystery* is reflective of my Heavenly Bodies poem, and the empowering human spirit, that greatest mystery of all. It also contains movements depicting that awakening vision. Other symbols in that composition suggested that one must delve down to the depth of human life in order to know that the spirit—animating life force—is the unifying force in all of nature.

In 2003 I began to write in earnest. The result was my 2006 first published book: *Of Golden Frogs and Such, A Story of Survival and Transformation*. It is a memoir that was necessary to resolve the wounds encountered in my family and that evil psychologist, as well as giving meaning to my brother's life. It also served to strengthen my voice, for the power of voice is inextricably combined with one's sense of self-worth. That book evoked a sense of privacy I had never known before: there is no personal god that knows one's every thought and feeling; no human, including a psychologist/psychiatrist can know what is in another's mind.

Continual research and evolution of consciousness resulted in three more published books—a process of abstracting the residual threads of religious myth and human constructionism so woven into my mind.

The second book, *The Emergent Mind: Evolution, The Wisdom of Nature*, was inspired by Sperry's works. A major mistake in that book was being drawn, by a female psychiatrist, into the myth of precognition, the supernatural capacity to know the future. That myth was applied to a strange piece of prose, *My Golden Frog*, written within a brief two hour period in April, 1993. That prose seemed to come through me, not from me. It was the discovery of my own unconscious, the source of its dictation. It was, essentially, a self-fulfilling prophesy: "a prediction that directly or indirectly causes itself to become true, by the very terms of the prophecy itself, due to positive feedback between belief and behavior."[72]

That writing contained unconscious knowledge of the dual brain's functioning as well as that contra-lateral arrangement, evident in the words, "my eyes, open to separate worlds." It contained, symbolically, my unconscious disgust with the field of psychology and the revelations encountered by working with clients, especially grief, necessary to bring resolution to the wounds from one's past. It eventually became obvious that "to feed the starving soul," the ending of that prose, foreshadowed my writing, as well as its purpose: to nurture the human spirit in others.

Due to that major mistake—the myth of precognition—*The Emergent Mind* was removed from reproduction and replaced with

Flatland, Spaceland, and Beyond: The Wisdom of Nature. Abbott's *Flatland, A Romance of Many Dimensions,* was used as a metaphor to introduce the multidimensional human. I had discovered that book during research of the concept of dimensions in order to understand the meaning of that awakening vision, which was turning my life inside out and upside down. I was fortunate to find a single copy of the original 1894 revised edition at the Winter Park library. It brought to light the multi-dimensional reflective human already conceived in 1994, not only the capacity to self-reflect but a reflection of all of nature.

The ending of that book was a poem which had been evoked by a new composition, *Ode to Being*:

Through space and time
I stand undaunted
in the guiding light
of all nature.

Gone, the chains
of human myth;
free to be
all that I am.

The joy that
freedom brings
grows richer
each day,

Extolling harmony
and the gift of life.
Ever rising
is true Being.

My last book, *Empowered Humans: The Phenomenon of Being*, was published in 2016. As said in the Introduction, it is described as a holistic treatise on the human potential for wholeness and balance. It is knowledge shared by example, for I had realized that it is impossible to know all the environmental differences that affect another's life. It includes a more detailed version of my experiences and evolution of consciousness. The person I am today barely resembles the divided person I was over a quarter of a century ago. Comparing my initial writings, including my biography, with *Empowered Humans* can be likened to comparing a rotary telephone with an iPhone 10, yet to be invented.

That book also answered a question I had been asking for years regarding my creative illness and subsequent awakening—Why me? Now I know it was multidimensional: I found comfort in the wonder and beauty of nature, even as a child. Learning to play piano as a child contributed to my even brained oddity. The classical music I learned to play has been mentally and spiritually therapeutic throughout my life. A bond formed with my baby brother, six years younger, was an early arousal of the mother instinct to nourish and protect the young, resulting in devotion to the well-being of my beloved daughter and my motivation for change. That bond of love and compassion also influenced my decision to become a mental health counselor, as well as my creative illness. The phenomenal wisdom in Longfellow's *A Psalm of Life*, found when I was a teenager, also remained in my subconscious mind.

One inspiration for *Empowered Humans* was another composition, *Transitions in Space and Time: The Ascending Power Within*. When I began to write those sounds in my mind, they seemed extraordinarily familiar. Out of curiosity, I dug through my stack of discarded compositions and discovered that it had already essentially been written seventeen years before in two separate songs,

Colors and *Death of Narcissus.* Another dimension of my sense of purpose—to promote personal growth and development—manifested in my own flowering, bringing to actual my whole self.

Another inspiration was a major insight—there is a test for truth. Like authenticity, it is the same backward and forward in time; the same from the inside out, the outside in, from the bottom up and the top down. I also learned that details are just as important as that holistic view in order to substantiate truth.

It is still remarkable to me that self-discovery regarding the creative spatial brain attributes, as well as the multiple dimensional human, gained through experience and insight, preceded knowledge from without. Yet research resulted in validation. Contained in this writing are the resources for that validation, which helped me to bring clarity to internal knowledge. Having progressed even further, through continual research and contemplation, I have made minor corrections as well as given credence to and expanded knowledge regarding those resources, which have fulfilled the test for truth.

Self-knowledge, including the fundamental nature of humans, is, indeed, the pathway to freedom. Like Hawking said, "In my mind I am free."

Another insight has been achieved in this writing. If knowledge attained through the content of the first four chapters had been available to me in the field of psychology, the many years of overcoming the man-made impediments, including that evil psychologist, would have been reduced to a much briefer period, perhaps even months. I am hopeful that this writing will offer the gift of time to those who choose self-knowledge—the path to freedom and wholeness—and/or to fulfill Gandhi's directive to BE the change so sorely needed in this world.

It will not only result in positive change regarding one's personal functioning but can influence the non-complacent people within one's environment through respect for their lives and encouraging self-knowledge. Essentially one would also accomplish what Longfellow refers to as leave "footprints on the sands of time." (Appendix II) Those footprints would eventually evidence Roger Sperry's conclusion—human values become the underlying key to world change.

The change from materialism to wholistic humanism can definitely produce a more unified and balanced human world, reflective of the harmony of nature.

Appendix I

Auditory-Sequential and Visual-Spatial learning[73]

The Auditory-Sequential Learner	The Visual-Spatial Learner
Thinks primarily in words	Thinks primarily in pictures
Has auditory strengths	Has visual strengths
Relates well to time	Relates well to space
Is a step-by-step learner	Is a whole-part learner
Learns by trial and error	Learns concepts all at once
Progresses sequentially from easy to difficult material	Learns complex concepts easily; Struggles with easy skills
Is an analytical thinker	Is a good synthesizer
Attends well to details	Sees the big picture; may miss details
Follows oral directions well	Reads maps well
Does well at arithmetic	Is better at math reasoning than computation
Learns phonics easily	Learns whole words easily

Can sound out spelling words	Must visualize words to spell them
Can write quickly and neatly	Much better at keyboarding than handwriting
Is well organized	Creates unique methods of organization
Can show steps of work easily	Arrives at correct solutions intuitively
Excels at rote memorization	Learns best by seeing relationships
Has good auditory short-term memory	Has good long-term visual memory
May need some repetition to reinforce learning	Learns concepts permanently; does not learn by drill and repetition
Learns well from instructions	Develops own methods of problem solving
Learns in spite of emotional reactions	Is very sensitive to teachers' attitudes
Is comfortable with one right answer	Generates unusual solutions to problems
Develops fairly evenly	Develops quite asynchronously (unevenly)
Usually maintains high grades	May have very uneven grades
Enjoys algebra and chemistry	Enjoys geometry and physics
Masters other languages in classes	Masters other languages through immersion
Is academically talented	Is creatively, technologically, mechanically, emotionally or spiritually gifted
Is an early bloomer	Is a late bloomer

Appendix II

A Psalm of Life by Henry Wadsworth Longfellow

THE FOLLOWING RENDITION has been altered to reflect this author's beliefs.

Tell me not in mournful numbers,
Life is but an empty dream!
For the soul is dead that slumbers,
And things are not what they seem.

Life is real! Life is earnest!
And the grave is not its goal;
[But to bring nourishment
To one's empowering soul.]

Not enjoyment, and not sorrow
Is our destined end or way;
But to act, that each tomorrow
Find us farther than today.

Art is long, and Time is fleeting,
And our hearts, though stout and brave,
Still, like muffled drums, are beating
Funeral marches to the grave.

In the world's broad field of battle,
In the bivouac of Life,
Be not like dumb, driven cattle!
Be a hero in the strife!

Trust no Future, howe'er pleasant!
[Grieve the past and] bury its dead!
Act, - act in the living Present!
[Spirit within, and cosmos] o'erhead!

Lives of great men all remind us
We can make our lives sublime,
And, departing, leave behind us
Footprints on the sands of time;

Footprints, that perhaps another,
Sailing o'er life's solemn main,
A forlorn and shipwrecked brother,
Seeing, shall take heart again.

Let us then be up and doing,
With a heart for any fate;
Still achieving, still pursuing,
Learn to labor and to wait.

ENDNOTES

Introduction

1. Britt, Laurence W., *Free Inquiry magazine*, Volume 23, # 2 (Spring, 2003) found at website http://occupyoakland.org/2012/02/fascism-anyone-the-14-defining-characteristics-of-fascism-by-laurence-w-britt/

2. http://www.merriam-webster.com/dictionary/complacency

3. Sperry, Roger W., *Mind, Brain, and Humanist Values,* U. Chicago Press, 1965. This Article can be found at http://people, uncw. edu/Puente/sperry/sperrypaters/60s/125-1966.pdf.

4. Gleick, James, *Chaos: Making a New Science*, Penguin Books, 1988

5. Szasz, Thomas S., M.D., *The Myth of Mental Illness, Foundations of a Theory of Personal Conduct*, Harper and Row, 1974

6. Ellenberger, Henri F., *The Discovery of the Unconscious: The History and Evolution of Dynamic Psychiatry*, Basic Books, 1970

7. Jung, Carl G., *Man and His Symbols*, Dell Publishing, 1968

8. Edwards, Betty. *Drawing on the Right Side of the Brain*, Jeremy P. Tarcher/Putnam, 1989 An expanded and updated edition was published in 1999: *The New Drawing on the Right Side of the Brain*, is a product of Betty Edwards' evolving thought.

9. www.thefreedictionary.com/wisdom

Chapter 1

10. Gould, Stephen Jay, *The Mismeasure of Man*, W. W. Norton & Co., 1981

11. Ellis, Eugenia Victoria, and Reithmayr, Andrea G., *Claude Bragdon & the Beautiful Necessity*, Cary Graphic Arts Press, Rochester Institute of Technology, Rochester, New York, 2010. "Darwinian inequities" is a phrase used in Chapter 6, Architecture and the "Spirit" of Democracy, referring to the classification of people resulting in the toxins of a materialistic and fractious society.

12. *Zeitgeist, The Movie*, 2007 Documentary

13. Paine, Thomas, *The Age of Reason*

14. http://en.wikipedia.org/wiki/Bertrand_Russell

15. Meyer, Marvin, *The Gnostic Gospels of Jesus*, Harper Collins Publishers, 2005

16. Campbell, Joseph, *The Hero With a Thousand Faces*, New World Library, 2008

17. Arcones, Pedro Ccinos, *Matriarcado en China: madres, reinas, diosas, chamanes*, Madrid, 2011

18. Huang, Alfred, *The Complete I Ching*, Inner Traditions, 1998

19. Kevles, Daniel J., *In the Name of Eugenics: Genetics and the Uses of Human Heredity*, Harvard University Press, 1995

20. http://www.authorama.com/flatland-1.html

21. Ellis, Eugenia Victoria, and Reithmayr, Andrea G., *Claude Bragdon & the Beautiful Necessity*, Cary Graphic Arts Press, Rochester Institute of Technology, Rochester, New York, 2010

22. Banchoff, Thomas F., *Beyond the Third Dimension: Geometry, Computer Graphics, and Higher Dimensions*, Scientific American Library, 1990

23. *Plato, Five Great Dialogues*, Walter J. Black, Inc., 1969

24. http://www.merriam-webster.com/dictionary/millenarianism

25. Berger, Peter L., *The Sacred Canopy*, Anchor Books, 1969

26. http://dictionary,com/browse/socialconstructionism

27. Maguire, Daniel C. and Shaikh, Sa' Diyya, *Violence Against Women in Contemporary World Religions*, The Pilgrim Press, 2007

28. Farmer, Paul, *Pathologies of Power: Health, Human Rights, and the New War on the Poor*, University of California Press, 2005

29. Kidder, Tracy, *Mountains Beyond Mountains: The Quest of Dr. Paul Farmer, A Man Who Would Cure the World*, Random House, Inc., 2003 The quoted sentence is on the back cover of Tracy Kidder's book, a biography of Paul Farmer.

Chapter 2

30. www.thefreedictionary.com/insight

31. Sommers, Christina Hoff, and Satel, Sally, M.D. *One Nation Under Therapy: How the Helping Culture is Eroding Self-reliance*, McMillian, 2006

32. Thornton, Bruce S., <u>*Commentary*</u>, *October, 2005, Article,* Preview of *One Nation Under Therapy: How the Helping Culture Is Eroding Self-Reliance* by Christina Hoff Sommers and Sally Satel

33. Voneida, Theodore J., *A Biographical Memoir*, National Academies Press, 1997, available at www.nasonline.org

34. http://www. En.wikipedia.org/wiki/Roger_Wolcott_Sperry

35. https://en.wikipedia.org/wiki/Activity-dependent_plasticity

36. Mobbs, Dean and Watt, Carolyn, *Trends in Cognitive Sciences*, 15 (10), 2011

37. Sperry, Roger W., *Holding Course Amid Shifting Paradigms*, From proof for <u>The Metaphysical Foundation of Modern Science:</u>

Issues of Causality. Eds. W. Harman and J. Clark, Institute of Noetic Sciences (in press, 1994) This Article can be found at: people.uncw.edu/puentel/sperry/papers/1994 (#282)

38. Voneida, Theodore J., *Roger Wolcott Sperry*, The National Academies Press, found at website: http://www.nap.edu/html/biomems/rsperry.html

39. www.merriam-webster.com/dictionary/fortitude

40. *New York Times,* Nov. 9, 1930

41. Capra, Fritjof, *The Science of Leonardo: Inside the Mind of the Great Genius of the Renaissance,* Double Day, 2007

42. http://www.thefreedictionary.com/continuum

43. http://thinkexist.com/quotes/albert_einstein/

44. *The I Ching or Book of Changes,* The Richard Wilhelm Translation rendered into English by Cary F. Baynes, Princeton University Press, 1997, Page 505

45. Brabezon, James, *Albert Schweitzer: A Biography,* G. P. Putnam's Sons, 1975

46. Morrison, Toni, *The Nobel Lecture in Literature, 1993,* Alfred A. Knopf, 1994

Chapter 3

47. Ellenberger, Henri F., *The Discovery of the Unconscious: The History and Evolution of Dynamic Psychiatry*, Basic Books, 1970

48. Sperry, Roger W., *Mind, Brain, and Humanist Values*, from Platt, John R. *New Views of the Nature of Man*, U.Chicago Press, 1965

49. Jung, Carl G., *Man and His Symbols*, Dell Publishing, 1968

50. Chesler, Phyllis, *Women and Madness*, Harcourt Brace Jovanovich, 1989

51. Pinker, Steven, *How the Mind Works*, W. W. Norton and Co., 1997

52. Stout, Martha, *The Paranoia Switch*, Sarah Crichton Books, 2007

53. Gould, Stephen Jay, *The Mismeasure of Man*, W. W. Norton & Co., 1981

54. Frank, Jerome D. and Frank, Julia B., *Persuasion and Healing: A Comparative study of Psychotherapy*, John Hopkins University Press, 1991

55. Chesler, Phyllis, *Women and Madness*, Harcourt Brace Jovanovich, 1989

56. http://www.salon.com/2011/10/16/sybil_exposed_memory_lies_and_therapy/

57. McHugh, Paul, Book Review, <u>The Wall Street Journal</u>, June 29, 2008, reviewing Richard J. McNally's Book, *Remembering Trauma*, Belknap/Harvard, 2003

58. http://www.voxfux.com/features/cia_murder.html

59. Stewart, Ian and Joines, Vann, *TA Today*, Lifespace Publishing, 1987

60. Glasser, Howard, *Transforming the Difficult Child,* available on 2003 video at website, www.difficultchild.com

61. https://en.wikipedia.orgwiki/Gottfried_Wilhelm_Leibnix

Chapter 4

62. Edwards, Betty. *Drawing on the Right Side of the Brain*, Jeremy P. Tarcher/Putnam, 1989

63. https://www.wikipedia.org

64. http://www.pbs.org/programs/killer-stress/

65. www.the free dictionary.com/subconscious

66. Edwards, Betty, *The New. Drawing on the Right Side of the Brain*, Jeremy P. Tarcher/Putnam, 1999

67. Barnes, Tom, *Washington Post*, January, 8, 2015

68. Frank, Jerome D. and Frank, Julia B., *Persuasion and Healing: A Comparative study of Psychotherapy*, John Hopkins University Press, 1991

Chapter 5

69. Matthew 5:39: "But I say unto you, that ye resist not evil: but whosoever shall smite thee on the right cheek, turn to him the other."

70. http://www.wikipedia.org/wiki/Human_self-reflection

71. Brown, H. Jackson, Jr., *Life's Little Treasure Book ON WISDOM*, Rutledge Hill Press, 1994

72. https://en.wikipedia.org/wiki/Self-fulfilling_prophecy.

Appendix I

73. http://www.education.com/reference/article/Ref_Visual_Learner/